for the Love *of* Plants

for the Love *of* Plants

Adam Frost

**Over 150 plants to bring joy
to your garden and your life**

CONTENTS

FINDING YOUR WHY

"Warm Love" – Van Morrison

Just as music can drive emotions, connect people, and tell a story, a garden has the ability to evoke a feeling, bring people together, and create wonderful memories. Recently, while listening to music, what popped up? "Warm Love" by Van Morrison. The lyrics to this song are glorious and leave you with, as it says, "Warm Love." In early 2022, we moved to a house with a much smaller garden. The moment I walked into that garden, I felt connected. It became my safe place; it is my warm love.

Ever since I can remember, I have been drawn to music, even more so by lyrics, as words have a real impact on me. Maybe because I'm dyslexic, I can listen to songs and make sense of what is being said. I use music every day—I send Mrs. Frost or the kids a song as a way to express how I feel or to help them understand something they feel... I think they like it!

When I start talking about design, gardens, and music, my kids just smile at me. I'm sure they think I'm an old romantic fool—and maybe they are right. I think that's better than being old and cynical. Whenever I have designed gardens, I have always had music on in the background; I've even assigned every client an album or an artist who will drive their garden design. I rarely tell them—it just helps me with the process. As well as the atmosphere that the music creates, I use its rhythm and repetition to mirror how we move through our gardens: speed up, slow down, pause.

Anyway, isn't this book about plants? Well, yes, but I'm also trying to picture what this book would feel like—and, yes, I want it to feel like something, not just be a reference book (as useful as those are). Think of this book as an album, and each chapter as a song on that album.

For me, music and gardens are where I can go to connect or enter a different world: I can escape. I don't remember a time when I wasn't connected to plants—whether at the garden with my grandparents or as an apprentice at the Parks Department. Looking back, I realize my love for plants has evolved, even matured—like my marriage!—over my life and become more interesting—in fact, fascinating.

During the last few years, I have done a lot of thinking, which has dug up many memories—the good, the bad, and the indifferent! Interestingly, though, a lot of the good ones involve plants, and that's what I want to share here. We are living in very different times than when I was a lad down at the garden with my grandad, and my life with plants since then has been one big experiment—and continues to be. I will go into the ground only knowing a fraction of what I want to know, but I want to share that fraction, and my love for plants.

THE STORY BEHIND THIS BOOK

During lockdown, like so many, we as a family had our challenges. Mrs. Frost was not doing well, nor was our youngest daughter. Then, just as we got through that, I caught Covid and shut myself away for 10 days to quarantine. During my isolation, I started to feel disconnected, as if my life were unraveling. I spent a lot of time looking out the window at the vast garden I'd created, and the only thing that comforted me was music.

Lots of people watching *Gardeners' World* each week seemed to love seeing my garden over the seasons, yet all I could see, trapped in my room, was a long list of jobs that had to get done. In all honesty, I was working stupid hours to keep everything going and was starting to feel overwhelmed. When I eventually left the room, I spoke to a doctor, who diagnosed burnout and a sort of depression. So I found myself, with a psychiatrist, exploring, explaining, and questioning what had been going on in my life. I began to think long and hard about what was really important to me.

During my sessions with the psychiatrist, lots of stuff came out, particularly about my childhood, how I had loved gardening with my grandparents, how I left home at 16 to work in the Parks Department, then got a job with the late, great Geoff Hamilton, as well as the craziness of the RHS Chelsea Flower Show, TV work, and how all of this led me to where I am now. It dawned on me that the two consistent elements in my life have been music and plants.

It became obvious that to get back on track mentally, I needed to simplify my life, so we downsized to a cottage with a much smaller garden. It was like flipping a switch. Immediately, I started to connect with the space and create a new garden in what felt like a different world, both personally and professionally, inspired by the music and plants that I love.

Designing my new garden and starting from scratch made me think about the plants I wanted to include.

Over the years I've built up a collection of plants that work hard, and even though some of the varieties may change, essentially this group has been with me for decades. It's a bit like making friends and keeping them for life; I know I can call on all of them, even if I haven't spoken to them for years, and I'll instantly have that old connection.

All the plants I've included in this book are special to me for one reason or another. Often, I'll look at a plant and it will bring back strong memories of a person, a time, or a place. Bedding plants and fuchsias remind me of my friends at the Parks Department, while agave, cacti, yuccas, and succulents remind me of my Scruffy Nan. She and Grandad both had relatively ambitious jobs, but they were quite bohemian and had a garden that was a sort of overgrown wilderness, rather like the Lost Gardens of Heligan. Nan had loads of Belfast sinks full of plants that to me were like miniature worlds, and two aluminum greenhouses—one with succulents, cacti, and agaves, the other with coleus plants that I helped to propagate by taking cuttings. I realize now that Scruffy Nan was way ahead of her time, but the thing I remember most was a feeling of freedom when I was in their garden.

When I think about more classic veggie gardening, I'm with my Tidy Nan and Grandad. Their garden had the classic '70s striped lawn, edged by tiny borders, with a concrete path, clothesline, and greenhouse. I often think back to Saturday mornings when Grandad would put on his clip-on tie and jacket to go to the garden or go

Here I am with David Stevens at our RHS Hampton Court Flower Show design and construction stall.

blackberry picking. Of course, growing and foraging were important for people like my grandparents, who had experienced rationing during World War II.

I also used to help out on a farm when visiting my uncle, starting at six in the morning and working until late at night. I was found asleep in the grain truck more than once! My childhood was quite complicated, and I can now see that I created a connection to the outdoors and saw gardens and nature as places where I felt safe, where I could just be me.

As an adult, I've been lucky enough to be around some exceptionally talented and inspiring people. Geoff Hamilton was and continues to be a major influence. I started working for him when I was 21, when I thought I knew everything about everything. I had no idea then how ahead of the game he was. I learned all that I could from him; about our impact on our planet—the importance of using peat-free soil, about the work you need to put into creating good soil to make it the best growing material for plants, and organic gardening—and I started to wonder, what's this all about then? For Geoff, gardening was about finding balance, easing up on trying to control everything, and avoiding the use of chemicals.

Geoff taught in such an understated way, but you always sensed his vast knowledge. He had a quiet confidence, but he was fun, too, with a bit of naughtiness about him. It was Geoff and his son Nick who introduced me to herbaceous plants, cottage gardening, what plants meant, and what they could do. Geoff encouraged me to get into garden

design and sent me to train with the renowned landscape architect David Stevens, who also had a big influence on me. I remember coming back with some designs I'd come up with, one of which I called a Plantsman's Garden, another a Town and Country Garden. I showed them to him, nervous about his reaction, and he said, "So, where are you going to build those then? Go sort something out, and I'll come take a look." Being around people who create, and who care about what they do, made me aware that we can lose ourselves in the process and make something beautiful and practical. That's really special.

When Geoff died in 1996, his wife Linda gave me his spade, saying, "He saw something in you." This has always amazed me, as I couldn't have been easy to work with. I still really miss him. If there were two people whom I would love to see what I do now, it would be Geoff and Tidy Nan.

Plants continue to play a part in my relationships to this day, especially with my family. I love getting home and finding Sulina gardening in her jeans and a T-shirt and comparing it to the day I first met her, when she looked as if she'd just stepped off a makeup counter in a high-end department store. On our first date, she didn't know what a landscape gardener was, so it is particularly special to find her out there, getting into the gardening. I've also witnessed my daughter Abbie go on a little journey. When we were in the garden recently, I looked over, and she was happy as a pig in mud with her hands in the soil. Even Oakley, our youngest, is starting to dabble.

As a toddler in my great-great nan's garden, lending a hand!

I've got a tattoo on the side of my arm saying, "You may call me a dreamer," because that's what everybody called me. My dad used to tell me that I wasn't going to amount to anything because I was just a dreamer. Later on in life, I realized that in fact, the only thing that changes worlds is dreams.

I've come to realize there's not much that matters in life other than the people who are close to you, and nothing nicer than having the people you love most in the world enjoying the same stuff that you do. One of the most satisfying things I get out of my TV work is helping people become enthused about gardening and plants, and maybe making a difference in their lives. If you have the chance to improve a bit of the world and connect to it, do it!

When I was working as a landscaper, I was fortunate enough to construct gardens for some of the best designers around. I helped build a RHS Chelsea Flower Show garden for the late Terence Conran, and it was he who encouraged me to make the transition from building gardens to designing them. I had always wanted to understand this process, so I would deconstruct them in my head. That's weird, considering that now I sit in Chelsea show gardens and ad-lib about them to a TV camera. First, I look at the layout and hard landscaping, then the layers— trees, shrubs, herbaceous, etc.—then I put it all back together verbally. Over time I've learned that I can pretty much immediately know if a garden needs another tree or where the best place is to sit to watch the sun go down.

Somehow, I still have a child-like curiosity about stuff, and I love experimenting with new plants and finding different ways of doing things. There are lots of rules laid out in gardening books, and we've all got slightly different approaches, but if you listen to someone's point of view and keep an open mind, often you'll learn something. You don't have to agree with it, and you don't have to do it, but you may uncover useful information. For me, this is one of the reasons I find gardening really exciting. I reckon there's not a day when I don't discover something new.

I'm far more playful in my designs now than I've ever been, and probably far more honest, too. For me, every bed is a little piece of art, which together add up to a collection with lots of links running through them.

One of the biggest things I've learned to do is "read" a garden. Obviously, you have to understand the practicalities of the soil, the weather conditions, microclimates, and which plants will grow best, but increasingly, I try to analyze how a space makes me feel. And by that, I mean I really observe it, tune into its atmosphere, and understand why it makes you feel the way it does. How we respond emotionally to a garden is highly individual, but it should make you feel something as you step into it—whether good, bad, or indifferent. The way that the light moves through the space, the sounds, the view over its surroundings, the hard landscaping, textures, colors, climatic conditions, if it's damp or dry, windy or still, open or enclosed, the plants, the smells, the presence of wildlife should all stimulate you.

For me, the best gardens are those that are connected to their surrounding landscape, which is why it's so important to understand the setting before you plan your garden. If you take the time to walk or sit in your garden at different times of day and look beyond it, you'll understand it far better than by simply looking at it through a window or as a drawn-out plan. Invariably, good gardens are simply made of a series of different moments, whether of calm, excitement, sound, or movement, and those moments can be reflected in a song. We live in a world where often it's all about—bang!—let's have it now, but one of the beautiful things about gardening is its delayed satisfaction. So, let's not strive to have it all now—let's take our time and enjoy it moment by moment.

I've always loved a tractor—you can see the smile on my face!

Tidy Nan and Grandad with their black cat, Sooty, in my great-great nan's garden—you can see her cacti in her greenhouse behind.

STARTING ANEW

In essence, I created this new garden to work for my family—both aesthetically and practically—as well as for wildlife. In designing it, I listened to music to inspire me, to help me get the feel that I thought was best for each segment of the garden and how we would use it.

I have built personal relationships with so many plants over the years, and so in a way this garden has ended up being a massive journey down memory lane. I've made hundreds of gardens throughout my career, but this one has been created in a very different way. Here, it's been all about finding ways to really engage with the space and conjure up different atmospheres.

The design has been driven by emotions more than anything else, which is why you will see through the following chapters that each part of the garden has been given a corresponding song—one whose lyrics and rhythm reflect the atmosphere and moment I am trying to achieve in each area.

Creating this garden made me look at plants with fresh eyes, to really pay attention to the detail and how my choices individually and in combination make me feel. It's the first place where I've been confident to call myself a designer and to say this is what I do, this is how I do it, and this is what I get from it. I don't really care if people don't agree with me, but I hope a few might come along on the journey with me.

This is also the first time I've ever created a garden where there has been so much emphasis on environmental issues. These days, the conversation is all about sustainability, diversity, and creating habitats for wildlife, and although because of Geoff I've always gardened organically and done what I can to encourage beneficial insects, I now think even harder about why I'm using each and every plant.

Mine is not a big garden, but it still looks half-decent. I decided early on that the main focal point would be the plants, as I wanted the overall feel of the garden to be a thoughtfully made, hand-crafted space that I've filled with plants that I love. So, I've planted lots of stuff that I know will work, and a few different things that I'm experimenting with, which sit among them like little jewels. I've become more experimental with my plant palette in recent years, and I try to include a wide range of plants not just because of the changes in our climate but also because of the potential for new pests and diseases—so I'm not overly reliant on one group. And because I enjoy it.

My new garden is set out as interconnected spaces, which as a whole make up a sort of reversed L-shape. The design is such that you walk off the street, pass through a beautifully crafted wood gate and enter the front garden, where I've planted a mix of vegetables and ornamentals, fruit trees, and herbs. A gravel path takes you to a series of elongated steps, which helps slow you down to better appreciate the plants and leads to the front door around the side of the house and a shady garden. Moving around to the back of the house, you find the main garden, which is laid out over three to four terraced levels.

To maintain some continuity between the areas of the garden, I like to pick up vertical elements along the boundary—for example, a hedge or a tree—and repeat them throughout the space; it's easy on the eye and brings a sort of unity. There's something comforting and reassuring about repeat planting; it's a bit like having music on in the background while you work—it's kind of there but not there.

Having a consistency of materials is another way to bring a sense of cohesion to the garden and is also easy on the eye. One of the concepts that has really helped me with this is the idea that "less is more," so I've kept the materials and design quite understated. I've used wood for the front, side, and back gates, as well as for the edges of the main vegetable bed. The hard surfaces are mostly sandstone, with some limestone for the verticals, and the paths are all made from local gravel. I like the fact that all the materials feel connected to the region and tie back to those of our stone cottage, which dates back to the 1850s. The hard landscaping is practical and does what it needs to do, but it also doesn't jump out at you, which ensures that the emphasis remains on the plants.

It seems to me that nowadays, gardens are working much harder than they ever have before. You can make gardens that provide vegetables, fruit, and habitats for wildlife that also look really beautiful—it's just that sometimes, you need to think outside of the box to achieve this. And it's not just about how we plant our gardens but also how we maintain them.

I haven't made this garden in a hurry, and I have thought a lot about what is important to me and my family while planning the space and how we use it. We're all so obsessed with outward appearances, but actually what touches your emotions and makes you happy is far more important. This garden has been driven by that belief,

but to be honest, it could have been a window box, a small space, or a community project. It's not about the size of the garden—it's about finding whatever it is that works for you, what it is that you get from it. For me, it's not just the growing, the planting, and the taking care of it all; it's about the memories, friendships, or relationships that I have with other people because of the garden.

That's why I wanted to create different areas to go to, places to pause, to sit, to listen to music, or just to be, and for each area to have a distinct atmosphere. To open up our senses. Being able to come out to the office on a spring morning and have just five minutes with a bit of warmth from that eastern sun is pretty special. It's the same in summer, when, at the other end of the day, the setting sun has some warmth in it. Then, as the light starts to slowly fade, the whole mood of the garden changes.

More than anything else, this garden has been born out of sitting in the space and sketching ideas, playing with shapes and forms, and not fixing on anything too quickly. Writing this book was born out of the whole experience of starting this new garden, how it evolved, and the conversations I had with myself during the process.

Garden areas by song

1. Entrance
   "What a Wonderful World," Louis Armstrong
2. Front Garden
   "I Can See Clearly Now," Johnny Nash
3. Courtyard
   "Secret Garden," Bruce Springsteen
4. Lower Terrace
   "Lucky Man," Richard Ashcroft
5. Main Terrace
   "Mr. Brightside," The Killers
6. Gravel Garden
   "Wonderful Tonight," Eric Clapton
7. Upper Terrace Wrap and Greenhouse
   "Dreamy Skies," The Rolling Stones

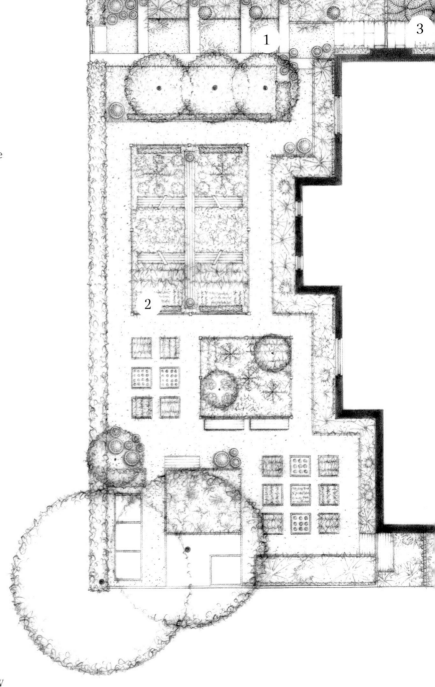

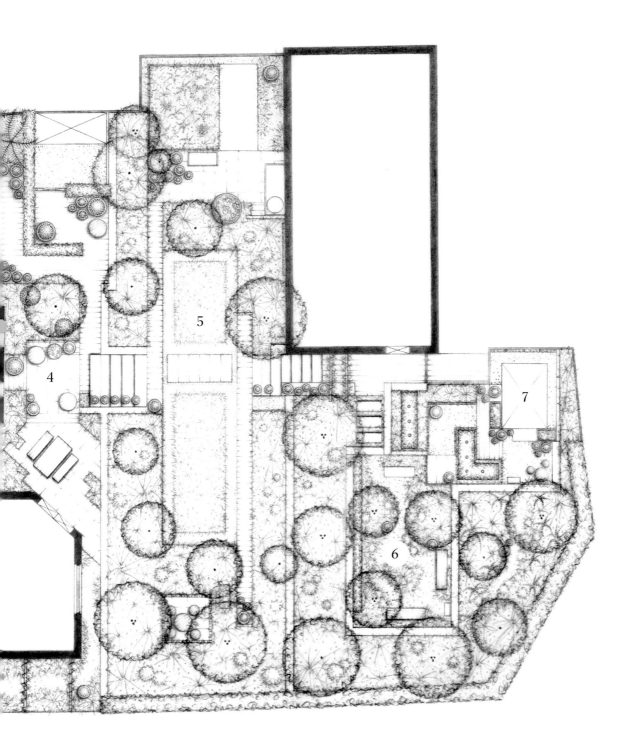

ENTRANCE

"What a Wonderful World"—Louis Armstrong

"What a Wonderful World" sets the scene. Imagine: It's Sunday morning, and the bells at the church down the road have just finished ringing. You enter the gate, the sun is on your back, a meadow waving on one side, fruit and herbs spilling over on the other, the large steps slow your movement and the world feels... well, wonderful!

It's easy to forget that your experience of a property doesn't necessarily begin the moment you arrive at the front door. I have to walk through my front garden to get to the house, so as well as making an impact, I wanted it to welcome visitors.

The entrance channels people into the house, so when someone arrives at the gate or one of the family comes home, it is important to me that what is in front of them is not just a visual experience but an emotional experience. So, when I designed this space, I first thought about how I wanted people to engage with it—physically, visually, and emotionally—for it to be an upbeat, joyful space, with a rhythm to it through the steps and planting, for it to say, "Hello, hope you're having a great day."

As you walk up the path from the gate toward the house, you're met by fanned fruit trees and herbs on your left, a mini meadow and orchard on your right, and a glimpse of the kitchen garden beyond. The tone is set. The garden is not just about beauty; it's also about habitat—feeding the family, but befriending the wildlife, too.

The garden slopes from the gate up to the house, so I have used a series of broad stone steps along the path (one step, couple of strides, one step, couple of strides, etc.) to slow people's movement as they approach. The stone slabs sit among gravel, which introduces a calming, crunching sound as you walk up the path. In summer, the meadow is alive with insects and birds, and the wildflowers reach head height when you enter the garden gate. As you walk up the steps, you begin to rise above the wildflowers, changing your view of the meadow.

Our house was once two limestone workers' cottages that were combined into one in 2005, and I assume that is when the Portugal laurel (*Prunus lusitanica*) hedging was planted along the boundary of the front garden, to separate it from the road. Given that the property dates to 1850, this choice of hedge was really jarring, especially as the house looks out onto a thirteenth-century church and its old chestnut trees, which must have been there for a very long time. So, I replaced the laurel with a yew hedge, which felt more complementary and timeless while still blocking the visual and noise pollution from the road.

So, arriving at the house should feel engaging—it sets a tone, and you think, "Oh, I'm in an orchard, and there's a little meadow. What's this all about?" It brings a smile to someone's face.

I do love a good pear! In early summer, thin out weaker fruit frequently so you get a better crop later in the season. As I was told as an apprentice, go back and do it again, because you won't have thinned enough the first time around.

EDIBLES BOUNDARY

The fruit trees along the boundary not only create a great backdrop for the planting below; they bring their own interest through the year and some softer screening for privacy, demonstrating the craft of gardening.

Traditionally, these front gardens would have been more open spaces, bounded by low fences, which is why I opted for the low fencing. However, to create a bit more privacy, along the boundary with my neighbor, I've run a pressure-treated timber picket fence that's secured to tall, 6½ft (2m) high posts, between which I've run evenly spaced horizontal wires. To these wires, I've tied some fanned fruit trees, which provide a filter without making the garden feel overly enclosed. Underneath the fanned fruit, the shrub structure is created by *Ugni* and *Rubus* with small *Taxus* domes that are repeated to drive movement as you walk up the steps. The shrubs are interplanted with herbs, making the most of the sunny spot and accessibility from the house. The herbs are subtle, with soft greens and small flowers that don't vie for attention, letting the fruit trees and meadow to the right of the path sing.

Planting the smaller herbs in between the *Taxus* domes.

Planting plan

Trees and Shrubs

- ● *Prunus* 'Jubilee'
- ● *Prunus* 'Stella's Star'
- ● *Prunus* 'Warwickshire Drooper'
- ● *Salvia rosmarinus* 'Miss Jessopp's Upright'
- ● *Rubus parviflorus* 'Bill Baker'
- ● *Taxus baccata* (dome)
- ● *Ugni molinae*

Perennials

- ○ *Agastache foeniculum*
- ● *Agastache rugosa* f. *albiflora*
- ● *Allium tuberosum*
- ● *Allium fistulosum*
- ● *Borago pygmaea*
- ● *Foeniculum vulgare*
- ● *Hyssopus officinalis*
- ● *Monarda fistulosa*
- ● *Origanum vulgare* 'Oregano'
- ● *Rumex sanguineus*
- ● *Salvia lavandulifolia*
-    *Thymus* 'Doone Valley'

Young fanned fruit in its first year of planting. This is a great way of dividing a space; placed along the neighbor's boundary, it provides a screen, but they can pick the fruit, too.

Fanned fruit boundary

While training fruit trees as fans creates a screen, you still get light filtering through and are able to have a conversation with the neighbors! In fact, I probably chat with the neighbors more in the front garden than anywhere else. I think sometimes we forget how important it is to connect with the people around us, and front gardens often get overlooked as sociable spaces. Also, it's nice that they can benefit from the fruit that hangs on their side of the fence. I have even had one or two delivery drivers asking if they could try a pear—how cool is that?

To create the fanned fruit boundary, I've run wires horizontally between supporting posts, starting at 16in (40cm) above the ground, repeating these upward with 12in (30cm) between them. I've tied some greengages, plums, and damsons to the wires, which I bought as bare-root trees in the winter, which means you get more for your money, as they are cheaper than buying potted plants. You can buy bare-root trees between November and March, while containers are available all year-round.

Herbs

In front of the fruit trees, I've planted a mass of herbs, which, although they look beautiful and ornamental, were, in fact, planted to satisfy our culinary needs. We use them all the time in cooking, so I've put them in an easily accessible spot, just a short walk down some steps from the front door. I've got all the classics, such as rosemary, thyme, oregano, and mint. It feels really special to use your own herbs, and it makes such a difference in cooking when they are freshly picked. As well as choosing them for their aromatic interest, I've played with shapes and forms rather than colorful flowers, introducing agastache and monarda plants for height and borage for texture. For further softness, I also let the herbs self-seed into the gravel path in front of the border.

Growing mint in containers rather than in borders will help control its growth and stop it from taking over!

Agastache foeniculum
Anise hyssop

Height 35in (90cm) **Spread** 16in (40cm)
Time of flower Summer **Soil** Rich and
fertile **Position** Full sun **Hardiness** Hardy
in a sheltered position

A really good, upright perennial herb.
The leaves have a nettle-like look and
carry an aniseed-meets-mint scent. The
plant holds its form well, its verticality
makes it really useful for interplanting, and
it provides late summer color. Each stem is
topped with dense bottle-brush-shaped
flowers that are dark blue/purple in color
and can carry into early winter, after which
the spikes turn dark brown and can hold
on until early spring, making it a valuable
addition to any border. It works well in the
sun and will deal with dry conditions, then
once established, it seems to tolerate cold
temperatures, as long as the ground is not
too wet. If I'm adding to a border, I tend
to plant earlier in the year so the plant
has some time to establish before the
winter, so if you do plant late in the season,
I would provide some protection against
frost. When the plant is flowering, bees,
butterflies, and birds will flock to it. The
leaves can be used fresh or dried and are
really useful in the kitchen to flavor meat
dishes, add to drinks, and make teas.

Allium tuberosum
Garlic chives

Height 20in (50cm) **Spread** 8in (20cm)
Time of flower Summer–early fall
Soil Moderately fertile, moist, well-drained
Position Full sun **Hardiness** Fully hardy

You will also hear these called Chinese
chives, and they are a close relative to
Allium schoenoprasum (chives), but rather
than the mild onion flavor, they carry
a sweeter garlic taste, especially if you
harvest regularly. Lovely mixed into salads!
Added to that, they are a little more showy
and work well as an ornamental. They
seem to do okay in most soils but do like
the sun to get the best from them. I have
grown them in a pot, which, if you can
keep frost-free, can be harvested through
the colder months, when chives are great
in stews and soups. Late summer is when
you will normally see the plant in full
bloom, covered in star-like white flowers
that are great for cutting. Put a few in
a jar, and the scent might surprise you—it's
more honey-like than onion-y. These sit
above flat gray-green leaves that have a
shine to them and a slightly rounded tip.
The plant clumps up well and is worth
using in larger groups if you have room.
Once the flowers are gone, black seeds
come to the fore, which are also edible.

Borago pygmaea
Pygmy borage

Height 12in (30cm) **Spread** 18in (45cm)
Time of flower Summer–fall **Soil**
Well-drained **Position** Full sun/partial
shade **Hardiness** Hardy

This is a little bundle of pure joy! So many
of us know *Borago officinalis* from our
summer drinks—well, this is a bit like that,
except it's shrunk in the wash, and every
detail has been intensified to create deep
green, small rosettes of bristly foliage,
which feel a little unshaven to touch. The
Romans and Greeks used borage, as it
was thought to provide courage in a battle,
and when I look at this little borage variety,
the leaves look tough and as if they could
survive anything! The slim, branched stems
carry small sky-blue, bell-shaped, nodding
flowers, which will hold for a good few
months. Like its larger cousin, the flowers
can be used in drinks and salads, and it is
also great for pollinators. I tend to plant at
the edge of borders and let it have its head
as it seeds well, and I also have it popping
up in a gravel path, where it looks great.

Hyssopus officinalis
Hyssop

Height 24in (60cm) **Spread** 31in (80cm)
Time of flower Summer **Soil** Most types
Position Full sun **Hardiness** Fully hardy

Another member of the mint family, this is a great border plant once it gets established. The stems are vertical and carry spikes of cracking tubular-shaped blue flowers in summer that can hold until early fall. Leaves are narrow and lance-like and have a silvery touch to them. The plant carries good aromatics, the leaves and flowers can be used in the kitchen, and I tend to use the latter more, which are great added to a salad and create a comment or two. It's also an antiseptic and a great cough reliever. This plant loves sunny, well-drained conditions, is a super source of nectar and produces large quantities of pollen, so you will see it covered in bees. If blue is not your color, you can find pink and white varieties. It's another herb that will make an interesting low hedge and will dry well for the house.

Monarda fistulosa
American wild bergamot

Height 30in (75cm) **Spread** 18in (45cm)
Time of flower Late summer **Soil** Moist but well-drained **Position** Full sun/partial shade **Hardiness** Hardy

Wild bergamot doesn't just look good; it's really useful in the kitchen and has become a bit of a go-to for me. It's a great way of adding a little citrus flavor in anything from tea to fish dishes, but it's not just good in the kitchen; it works well with ornamental grasses and other herbaceous plants. It carries lilac flowers that are surrounded by bracts of a pinkish tone. I always think they look like a woman's hat. These will dry and carry seedheads through the winter, which look amazing on a frosty morning. Stems are erect and carry oval, green-toothed leaves at regular intervals along the stems and are highly scented. You get tones of lemon and orange, and the plant forms a really good bush as the season moves on. It works in so many settings, being happy in full sun or partial shade in any good garden soil, as long as it it not too dry. One of its common names is bee balm, which more or less tells you that the bees, butterflies, and other pollinators love it. If wild bergamot does not do it for you, there are plenty of other hybrids and forms available.

Salvia rosmarinus 'Miss Jessopp's Upright'

Rosemary 'Miss Jessopp's Upright'

Height 3ft (1m) **Spread** 3ft (90cm) **Time of flower** Spring –early summer **Soil** Well-drained **Position** Full sun/partial shade **Hardiness** Hardy

I love the origins of the name "rosemary"—from the Latin *ros*, meaning "dew," and *marinus*, meaning "sea," so "dew of the sea," which tells you this plant is quite tough. The stories about rosemary are amazing; one of my favorites is its link with fidelity and love. (Mrs. Frost really doesn't understand what I'm trying to say when I bring a plant home!) Rosemary is a base requirement for any herb garden, and there are quite a few to choose from. I like 'Miss Jessopp's Upright' because of its vertical growth habit. I have grown it to over 3ft (1m), and you can even create a hedge from it. Like many other varieties, it has evergreen, needle-like leaves, and in spring, it is covered with pale sky-blue flowers loved by bees and other pollinating insects. Like many woody herbs, it benefits from regular cutting, which is a great way to keep its shape. I love making tea that can aid digestion, or you can throw leaves into the bath after a day in the garden to ease aching muscles! I think we all need a little more rosemary in our lives.

Thymus 'Doone Valley'

Thyme 'Doone Valley'

Height 4in (10cm) **Spread** 12in (30cm) **Time of flower** Summer **Soil** Moist but well-drained **Position** Full sun **Hardiness** Hardy

Doone Valley in North Devon is somewhere we used to go on vacation as kids and swim in the river. It is the first place I can remember having a cream tea (cream first, of course, it's Devon), and that alone is a good-enough reason to grow this little beauty. It's a variegated lemon thyme that has its value in the kitchen and a great little groundcover with foliage that is mainly dark green with near-golden markings. It bears clusters of flowers that are pinky-mauve in later summer, which contrasts well with the foliage and will hold for a long period, plus they are themselves edible. Thyme is native to the Mediterranean, so it loves a sunny spot in a lighter soil that does not need to be rich in nutrients—in fact, if it has to work a little harder, you will find it keeps a better shape. You only have to see it in the wild to understand how tough it is. Thyme seems to have been an important herb for centuries, and it's a bit of a go-to for me—so versatile in the kitchen, and it really lifts many dishes. If, like me, you are planting in slightly heavier soil, introducing some sand to the soil when planting will help. You may just find they don't live as long as they would in sandy soil, but that's okay with me. Lastly, like most herbs, they will work better if you are cutting them regularly.

Ugni molinae
Chilean guava/murtillo

Height 5–6½ft (1.5–2m) **Spread** 3ft (1m) **Time of flower** Spring–early summer **Soil** Well-drained **Position** Full sun/partial shade **Hardiness** Hardy to 14°F (-10°C)

There are two things that I know to be favorites of Queen Victoria: One is the wool from Ryeland sheep; the second, which is of far more use to us all, is the fruit of this evergreen shrub. And I can see why... When you pick the fruit, you do not expect it carry a wonderful perfume nor to carry a flavor of strawberry with a little vanilla edge! For me, they ripen at the end of the summer, into early fall. My favorite way of eating them is scattered over a bowl of yogurt—they are like peas of sweetness that just pop in your mouth. I also think they would make a good jam. The plants are evergreen and have small, leathery leaves with white-flushed flowers, and they look lovely in a group of pots. I first started growing it in a pot because I did not think it could handle the colder winters in my garden, but one year I forgot about it and left it out, and it was fine. So, I have now planted it in a sunny border protected by the fence, where it seems perfectly happy. It will tolerate a little drought once established, but a late frost may catch new growth, although I have found they usually recover well. If you live in a very cold region, it makes sense to provide some winter protection. My sheltered spot not only helps it though the winter but also encourages it to fruit. I do think if grown somewhere really mild, it would make a lovely hedge—I'm just waiting for that opportunity!

MINI MEADOW

To the right of the front gate is a retaining wall along which I've planted three wonderful, old pear trees and laid meadow turf, which is a beauty itself. It's not a large area, but it adds more diversity to the garden.

The sculpted pear trees come from an old Dutch orchard, and I've had them them for a few years—well, since the 2013 RHS Chelsea Flower Show. They are lovely pyramid forms. Mrs. Frost calls me a hoarder in that I never throw anything away, but you never know when something may come in handy, and I knew they would work somewhere!

To create the feeling I wanted, I opted to plant a meadow under the trees and some step-over apples on the vegetable garden side as a boundary. I could have gone down the route of researching native wildflowers, buying the seed, and mixing it myself, but I was in too much of a hurry. So, instead, I chose a generic meadow mix, but over time, I will do a bit more research and then add more plants, especially regional varieties. For starters, I've already added lots of bulbs, including daffodils (*Narcissus poeticus* var. *recurvus*), species tulips (*Tulipa turkestanica*), and camassias (*Camassia leichtlinii* 'Blue Candle'). Even after the first year of planting, and despite being small, the meadow is a stunning sight as you walk up the path, and I love the way people react to it.

It's fantastic that even in a small space, you can create diversity. It is reported that 97 percent of flower meadows have vanished since World War II, which breaks my heart, so it's good to be able to play a part in bringing back this particular sort of habitat.

Meadow mix plants
Achillea millefolium—Yarrow
Allium schoenoprasum—Chives
Centaurea scabiosa—Greater knapweed
Centaurea nigra—Common knapweed
Dianthus carthusianorum—Carthusian pink
Echium vulgare—Viper's bugloss
Filipendula ulmaria—Meadowsweet
Galium album (*Galium mollugo*)—Hedge bedstraw
Galium verum—Lady's bedstraw
Knautia arvensis—Field scabious
Leontodon hispidus—Rough hawkbit
Leucanthemum vulgare—Oxeye daisy
Linaria vulgaris—Toadflax
Lotus corniculatus—Bird's foot trefoil
Lychnis flos-cuculi—Ragged robin
Origanum vulgare—Wild marjoram
Plantago lanceolata—Ribwort plantain
Plantago media—Hoary plantain
Prunella vulgaris—Selfheal
Rhinanthus minor—Yellow rattle
Sanguisorba minor—Salad burnet
Silene dioica—Red campion
Silene vulgaris—Bladder campion
Veronica spicata—Spiked speedwell

Laying and caring for turf
Most meadow turf doesn't need much in the way of nutrients, but I did prep the ground really well before I laid mine, turning the soil with a fork and carefully removing weeds and roots. I knocked out any big lumps and picked out any larger stones, then ran a rake over the area to get a reasonably level bed. To lay the turf, in early spring, I placed it around the edge, then laid strips inside in a brick-like pattern, using planks to kneel on and avoid standing on the turf. Finally, I tamped it all down and gave it a really good watering. Within four weeks, it was all knitting together and beginning to grow.

I cut the turf with a hedge trimmer once a year when the flowers have died; in a bigger area, you could trim or scythe it. Always leave cuttings in situ for a few weeks to self-seed, then rake them up and add to the compost heap. Flowering plants in a meadow tend to ebb and flow; some years, certain plants might be stronger or drop off, but it's not something to worry about. However, if something really overrides the area, you might need to intervene.

The flowers will bloom differently
—some species will do better than others
over time. With a little help, the area finds
a happy medium.

Camassia 'Blue Candle'
Quamash/wild hyacinth

Height 28in (70cm) **Spread** 4–20in (10–50cm) **Time of flower** Spring–summer **Soil** Moist but well-drained **Position** Full sun/partial shade **Hardiness** Fully hardy

In North America, these plants grow in damp, grassy meadows, and as a rule, they do love those conditions, but as I don't live in the dampest spot in the country, I need to give them a little more care. Once it's got its roots in, it seems happy, and I have found 'Blue Candle' to be one of the easier bulbs for my area. It is fine in sun or partial shade, although I prefer to grow them in the latter, as the flowers last longer. It does look lovely under my pear trees in the mini meadow, where the light to mid-blue/purple flower spikes catch the eye rising up through the wildflowers. You can't help but fall in love! Their slightly later flowering means they carry bulb interest into May and June, plus they seem to draw in butterflies.

Narcissus poeticus var. recurvus
Old pheasant's eye

Height 16in (40cm) **Spread** 4in (10cm) **Time of flower** Spring **Soil** Most types **Position** Full sun/partial shade **Hardiness** Fully hardy

My childhood memories of daffs are of my nan more or less perched, waiting for them to go over, moaning about how untidy they were, then running out and folding the leaves in half before tying them up with string! She'd then turn to me and say, "That looks better, doesn't it?," to which I always wanted to shout, "No, Nan, it looks stupid!" But, being wiser than my years, I would, of course, just smile sweetly. We joked about it as I got older, when I would take her plants and make her promise not to tie them up. Bless her. Over the years, I have grown so many different narcissi, but I'm always drawn to *Narcissus poeticus*, known as the "poet's daff." It is a slightly later-flowering species of daffodil, with pure white, rounded petals that create a single flower with a small yellow cup with a thin red rim in the center. Something we sometimes forget about daffs is their scent; some are wonderful, and this falls into that bracket, where the fragrance is intense, and a small bunch will scent a room.

Tulipa turkestanica
Turkestan tulip

Height 8–12in (20–30cm) **Spread** 8in (20cm) **Time of flower** Spring **Soil** Light, well-drained **Position** Full sun **Hardiness** Fully hardy

There is something rather magical about tulips, and I have visited Holland many times over the years to enjoy the Dutch celebration of—or, some might say, obsession with—them. You only need to look back at the madness of tulip mania back in the seventeenth century for evidence of this. It is still hard to get your head around how this craze for tulips bankrupted so many people! All that said, I have always been drawn to the more delicate simplicity of the species tulips. Plus, you can just pop a few bulbs into the soil and forget about them! I think it was *Tulipa sylvestris* that first caught my eye, and it was the first one I ever grew—it's glorious. I call it "wet knees" because you are dropped to your knees by its scent, and watching the flower heads move in a spring breeze is mesmerizing! Anyway, *Tulipa turkestanica* is another one I love. It originates from the Mediterranean, all the way to the Far East, so it loves a sunny spot and a well-drained soil. It really is easy to grow, so much so that once it gets settled in, it can be quite a vigorous little thing, so it's fantastic for naturalizing in borders. It produces elegant, pointed, scrappy leaves that are a gray-green. Come mid-March, a series of stems emerge that carry star-like blooms that are ivory-white in color, with a deep yellow throat and a reddish flush on the outside of the flower. Species bulbs do tend to keep their flowers longer than the cultivars, but also the interest does not stop at the flower, as I think the seedheads are stunning too! There really is a natural elegance to these plants.

Camassia 'Blue Candle'

Narcissus poeticus var. recurvus

Tulipa turkestanica

FRONT GARDEN

"I Can See Clearly Now"—Johnny Nash

This garden is somewhere I spend a lot of time on the weekend, get my hands in the soil, and just go! I love growing for the family, and it's an area that just gives a sense of space. So, this is a part of the garden that sings "I Can See Clearly Now"!

The front garden is where I like to think things through, connect with the seasons, and try growing new plants. It seemed obvious that the very front section, which is south-facing and therefore sunny, would make a good kitchen garden. And as it's right next to the road, the passing traffic means it's not a place to sit for hours and relax (although there are far fewer cars on the weekend, which is when I spend more time out there), so it's perfect as a working plot.

These days, many of us lead busy lives, and even if we love gardening and cooking, we don't necessarily have a lot of time to dedicate to a stand-alone vegetable garden. So, I suppose the idea of having an ornamental kitchen garden is driven partly by the demands of modern living and partly by the incredibly fond memories I have of working with Geoff in the 1990s. I remember wondering then what planting ornamentals and veggies together was all about, until I learned that, actually, this method of gardening dates back to Medieval times. Now, I can see that it's perfectly possible to make a vegetable garden work aesthetically as well as provide food.

Gardeners have been training fruit since the early nineteenth century, and here I've planted fruit trees to make use of boundaries, walls, and beds in different forms—fanned, goblet, cordon, and step-overs—which looks beautiful and also draws a lovely parallel with the history of our house. I often wonder if trees were trained along this wall in times gone by. I like the idea that a part of the garden would have always been a proper working plot and that the people living here perhaps would have been growing their veggies in the same spot as I do. There is something really satisfying about having a sense of history and place, and it makes me feel like I belong here. I love that connection to the past.

By growing your own, you will start to think about food more seasonally, even if you supplement with store-bought ingredients. This will influence the way you shop; for instance, you may choose to only buy asparagus during the short window when it's in season. I also don't just see vegetable growing as something to feed the family—think of the memories you can create through simply tending the space. It's not important to be subsistent—it's all about Sunday mornings in the kitchen garden, nurturing and harvesting plants that we then get to cook and share as a family. If I can get a few great meals from what I grow, I'm happy!

The layout of the front garden is driven by the shape of the windows of the house. The borders along the south-facing wall offer more vertical growing space.

ORNAMENTAL KITCHEN GARDEN

For me, the idea of being able to grow food is quite magical. I still get a real thrill from sowing seed and caring for it and watching it grow, then cooking it and sharing it at the kitchen table.

I love trying to grow different veggies and fruits every year, and because the majority of vegetables are annuals, and seeds are relatively inexpensive, there's more freedom to really experiment year to year compared to gardening with ornamentals. I'm also fortunate that through my work, people send me stuff to try. Of course, in an ornamental garden, you could put in new plants, dig things up, and move them around, but normally you would create such a garden, then care for it, manage it, and guide it. With the veg garden, though, as it's in part an annual experience; you can think, "I'll give this a shot this year," but then change what you grow the next year. Also, what I love about kitchen gardening is the little and often nature of the work—I can more or less tend to it on a daily or weekly basis, depending on the season and how demanding the plants are.

Lots of edibles are also ornamental, such as Scots lovage (*Ligusticum scoticum*), which is a beautiful, strong, fleshy plant that gets to 16–20in (40–50cm) tall and looks great as an ornamental, but it can also be used in all sorts of dishes. I love the fact that if you show somebody a little leaf of silver-shield French sorrel (*Rumex scutatus*) and ask them what it is, most people won't have a clue, but then you ask them to taste it, they get a funny look, and they say, "Oh, it's a bit citrus-y." Eventually, they might come to the conclusion that it's some sort of sorrel. Seeing veg as useful and beautiful takes you on a journey and encourages you to think outside the box.

Another advantage of this sort of gardening is that the plants don't need as much watering, because by growing ornamentals and veggies together, you cover a lot more soil, which means less is exposed to the sun and, therefore, evaporation. You also inevitably end up companion planting, which means less risk of damage from pests and diseases. Growing ornamentals and veggies together can mean that some of the veggies get a bit long and leggy, but then when plants do start to fall over, they often have something to lean against to support them, and the top growth is absolutely fantastic. You just cut that off to eat and it's good—so what's the worry?

Designing the ornamental vegetable garden
In terms of the layout of my front garden, the house has some beautiful lines off it, so I just use these as guidelines to create a grid for a mix of straight vegetable beds alongside mixed beds. Initially, I set out the central space as a veggie garden, but later I divided that bed into six, with three beds running parallel to the yew hedge and the road, two beds deep. I used the cross bars on the windows as a repeat pattern on the ground to connect the architecture and the garden. At either end, I've planted more step-over apples, which help tie together the mini meadow and ornamental kitchen garden. Step-over varieties are a great way to yield fruit from small spaces. The four corner beds are interplanted with edibles

Planting Plan

Trees and Shrubs

● *Malus domestica* 'James Grieve' (Goblet)

◐ *Ribes odoratum* 'Dorothea's Early'

Perennials

● *Agastache rugosa* f. *albiflora*

○ *Allium tuberosum*

● *Borago officinalis*

● *Dahlia* 'Bishop of Llandaff'

○ *Dahlia* 'My Love'

◐ *Dahlia merckii*

● *Foeniculum vulgare*

● *Fragaria* × *ananassa* 'Marshmello'

○ *Ligusticum scoticum*

◐ *Melissa officinalis*

● *Origanum* 'Hot and Spicy'

○ *Origanum laevigatum* 'Herrenhausen'

◐ *Rheum* × *hybridum* 'Timperley Early'

◐ *Rubus arcticus*

◐ *Rumex scutatus* 'Silver Shield'

◐ Vegetables

Drifts

Narcissus 'Martinette'

Narcissus 'Sweetness'

Narcissus 'Sailboat'

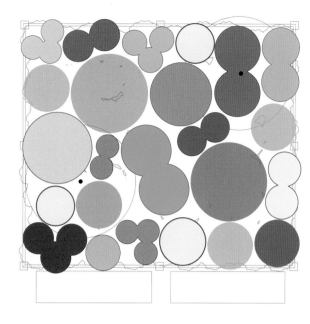

and ornamentals, while in the two central beds, I've focused on annual vegetables, growing asparagus down the middle to break these two beds into four smaller sections, creating a soft, feathery divide. It's nice looking out the windows and seeing the shapes repeated, and although fairly subtle, it does make the design feel comfortable in the setting.

To the right of the central bed is a wood-edged bed that is more of an ornamental kitchen garden. This is an area that has been designed in layers first, starting with two apple trees, grown as goblet shapes diagonally across the bed, slightly offset. Next, the shrub layer consists of woody fruit, including various blackcurrants and gooseberries, which form mounded bushes. Then, I worked through taller herbs, with the likes of fennel and agastache, before

adding ornamentals for spots of color. In this bed. I opted for dahlias, as Mrs. Frost loves them as cut flowers for the house, but you could use any flowers you like. I don't lift these dahlias over the winter—just give them a really good mulch to protect them from the cold.

Next, I included some of the lower-growing herbs—Scot's lovage, silver sorrel, oregano, alliums, and strawberries as groundcover—to provide both lovely fruits and beautiful flowers. I made sure to leave gaps for annual vegetables, such as kale, spinach, garlic, and beans. I have also planted various narcissi for some winter color, which just come up and do their thing, then once they're finished, the surrounding plants fill the space. What's good is that they are planted fairly close to the window, so we get to see them looking nice and cheerful early in the year.

A bird bath is tucked away in the ornamental kitchen border and can be viewed from the front sitting room.

As with all my designs, I have simply used various layers of interest, including trees, shrubs, herbaceous plants, and bulbs. Any gaps in the herbaceous layer leaves the opportunity to plant some annuals, which might be vegetables or herbs. These areas will no doubt evolve over time—yes, the structural planting will stay, but other parts will change as I come across plants to try.

In addition to the central beds, I've brought with me from my previous house Corten steel beds, which I've peppered through the space.

As a focal point, I've got a little potting shed, which you get a glimpse of as you enter the front gate and look to the far right across the mini meadow and veggie garden. I've also managed to work in a little bird bath and bird table. I was sitting in our back room that looks out onto the front garden and I could see a gap, so I found an old stone bird bath and put it under the tree, and now the birds come in and bathe in it, which helps bring the garden to life. I don't tend to cut anything back over the winter, so I end up with seedheads of plants like fennel, agastache, and lime balm,

and not long after I'd put in the bird bath, I was looking out the window on a nice, quiet, sunny Sunday morning, and something caught my eye. There were about 20 goldfinches darting in and out of the bed, pillaging the seedheads of the herbs! I sat and watched for ten minutes or so. It's a reminder that this is what it's all about, that this is what I'm chasing. Mrs. Frost doesn't like that it looks a bit messy out there at times, but for those few minutes, the garden was magical. And it's the way forward.

This shows that this style of gardening definitely helps to bring wildlife into the garden—and in the first year, we had a couple of hedgehogs running around. I think that's because front gardens tend to have picket fencing with lots of gaps, so the hedgehogs and other wildlife can work their way around them from garden to garden. Interestingly, although you might think it would be dangerous for hedgehogs to be so close to the road, actually all the cottages have stone walls at the front, so as long as the gates are closed, Mr. and Mrs. Hedgehog can safely run all the way across the front gardens on our street.

Agastache rugosa f. albiflora
Korean mint

Height 3ft (1m) **Spread** 18in (45cm) **Time of flower**
Summer–early fall **Soil** Well-drained **Position** Sun
Hardiness Fully hardy

This is probably my favorite of the agastache, although
I can't really say it is always reliable, as it can suffer if
we have a cold year. All that said, I do love the white
bottlebrush flower spikes that can reach to 6in (15cm)
long and arrive in midsummer, lasting well into early fall.
The spent flower stems hold good winter form, and the
bees and butterflies love them! The stems carry leaves
along their full length and bear a wonderful aromatic
scent. The leaves have an anise-like flavor that can be
beneficial in the kitchen. It is a plant that provides great
verticality to a border and seeds around nicely for me.
Lastly, it is said to be a great hangover cure—not that I
would I know! It also cuts well for the house. It loves a
sunny, well-drained position but can handle a little shade
if the soil is good.

Allium chinense
Chinese onion

Height 8–12in (20–30cm) **Spread** 3ft (1m) **Time of
flower** Fall **Soil** Well-drained **Position** Full sun **Hardiness**
Hardy

I think the Chinese onion is an allium that a lot of us
miss out on, and I'm not really sure why the leaves can't
be used in the same way as chives. I first saw and ate
this plant in Asia, where it is a staple vegetable. It is said
to have medical properties, too. The bulbs and leaves are
dried and pickled and eaten in different ways. The leaves
have a sweet smell to them, but it's the later rose-pink
flower that I really enjoy, because come late September
and into October, you see the arrival of attractive,
well-populated rose-pink seedheads. I have found the
leaves to be evergreen most years. I think the key to
success with this plant is a well-drained sunny spot, but
I have seen it growing in soils of varying fertility.

Agastache rugosa f. albiflora

Allium chinense

Dahlia merckii

Dahlia merckii
Merck dahlia

Height 5ft (1.5m) **Spread** 3ft (90cm) **Time of flower** Summer–fall **Soil** Rich and fertile **Position** Full sun **Hardiness** Hardy in a sheltered position

Dahlias have come in and out of fashion during my time, but I'm pleased to say they are back in the limelight for now, and it would be hard to find one that did not generate a smile. I grow dahlias in pots and in the ground, and I do mulch and protect a few, but not all, which means in a bad winter, I might lose a couple. While not great, it does make room for new ones, but don't tell Mrs. Frost! It's a close call, but I think *Dahlia merckii* is my favorite dahlia. It is hardier than most, with a single, simple flower that it produces en masse until late fall in a soft lavender-pink with a gold-rimmed center. The flowers arch on tall, wispy, red-tinged stems that rise well above soft green foliage. I have lost a good few hours in summer watching the bees in and around the open flowers. They are fairly low maintenance, but in a dry year, don't let them dry out completely, as they do tend to collapse. Deadhead regularly, and they will keep going until late fall/early winter, when I cut them back and cover the crowns with a good layer of composted bark.

Foeniculum vulgare
Common fennel

Height 5–6½ft (1.5–2m) **Spread** 20in (50cm) **Time of flower** Summer **Soil** Moist but well-drained **Position** Full sun **Hardiness** Fully hardy

Fennel has to be one of the most ornamental culinary herbs, and it has been used for centuries. You see it all over the globe, growing happily in the wild. It interplants well and is a super foil for other planting, producing masses of soft, lush, finely divided foliage with a feather-like quality. Bright green in color, the leaves carry a wonderful aniseed scent and taste. The yellow heads are like wild chervil flowers and last into late summer, when the aromatic seeds arrive. I don't find them to be the longest-living plants and tend to replace them every few years. It is really easy to grow from seed, so in the second or third year, collect a few seeds and start your next plants. This is a plant that hover flies seem to be partial to, and if the seedheads are left, they will provide food for the birds in the winter. It's really useful in the kitchen; all parts are great mixed with salad leaves, in soups, and worked through pasta. We also use it with fish. The seeds are great for flavoring when dried.

Foeniculum vulgare

Ligusticum scoticum

Ligusticum scoticum
Scots lovage

Height 28in (70cm) **Spread** 16in (40cm) **Time of flower** Summer **Soil** Rich and fertile **Position** Full sun/partial shade **Hardiness** Hardy in a sheltered position

I'm surprised you don't see this plant all over—it's a good one. It's not lovage as we know it; this variety is quite unusual, a native perennial that's compact and forms clumps of thick, satin, toothed leaves. The stems are reddish-green and carry umbels of tiny white flowers that appear in early summer. These flowers are edible, as are the seeds, which ripen to near golden in color. I love to eat them straight from the plant. If you are going to use it in the kitchen, go easy, as it does carry a strong flavor. It seeds really well for me, and I do sometimes let it self-seed freely in gravel areas! This plant loves the sun but will still work in partial shade. It's not just a great herb; it also really brings something to the border, so give it a shot, and you will soon see flowers covered with pollinators.

Melissa officinalis 'Lime Balm'
Lemon balm 'Lime Balm'

Height 28–35in (70–90cm) **Spread** 3ft (1m) **Time of flower** Summer **Soil** Moist but well-drained **Position** Full sun/partial shade **Hardiness** Hardy

This perennial herb is part of the mint family, and although it looks fairly similar to mint, the leaves have a distinctive smell of lime. It shares many characteristics with its cousin lemon balm in that it is robust and easy to grow. Originally from southern Europe and the Mediterranean region, 'Lime Balm' will tolerate most soil types, but it prefers a well-drained site in full sun or partial shade. During the summer months, it produces small creamy-white or pale purple flower spikes that are full of nectar and attract bees—hence the name *Melissa*, Greek for "honey bee." This plant will add a lime zing to cooking in general, and it has many uses in the kitchen; it can be infused to make teas as well as flavor ice cream, and it is also used as a herb for stuffing poultry. It is a useful addition to the herb garden, and if you harvest throughout the summer by snipping or pinching out the growing tips, it will keep regenerating all summer. The leaves can also be crushed and rubbed onto the skin to repel insects.

Melissa officinalis 'Lime Balm'

Origanum 'Hot and Spicy'

Origanum 'Hot and Spicy'
Oregano 'Hot and Spicy'

Height 2in (50cm) **Spread** 2in (45cm) **Time of flower** Summer **Soil** Loam, chalk, sand, free-draining **Position** Full sun **Hardiness** Fully hardy

Oregano is a close relative of marjoram and a lookalike, so they are sometimes confused, but marjoram is sweeter and lacks the spicy kick of oregano. I'm not sure why this plant is not sold more than it is. You will see varieties like 'Hopleys' and 'Herrenhausen', which both have their merits, but this is a dream! It was known as the joy of the mountain by the ancient Greeks, and that aromatic scent just carries me to the Mediterranean. It seems happy oin the poorest of soils and works really well in a gravel garden, where it looks at ease baking in the sun, but it's also happy in partial shade. It is a really good addition to the ornamental kitchen garden. It is nice to find a twist on the original, and 'Hot and Spicy' is just that. Oregano is a great addition to the kitchen; try it sprinkled on a summer tomato salad. The wiry stems carry white flowers throughout the summer above small, oval leaves with a matte finish. It's also a super little ornamental filler. It's happy in a pot as long as it doesn't get too wet, especially in winter.

Narcissus 'Martinette'

Narcissus 'Martinette'

Height 12–16in (30–40cm) **Spread** 16in (40cm) **Time of flower** Spring **Soil** Moist but well-drained **Position** Full sun **Hardiness** Hardy

I think there is something rather special about cutting daffs for the house—quite simply, they make me smile! I have a mix of sizes and colors in the front garden, but I think 'Martinette' is my favorite, not just because of its flower, which is a dainty little thing, but because its scent carries a real punch of sweet and musky fragrance. As happy in pots as in long grass, multiple flowers are produced on single stems with gray-green leaves, each with soft yellow petals and rich orange cups. It's not too fussy when it comes to soil—it just needs reasonable drainage, and it seems to love my more limey conditions. Mine flower a little later and last well into later April, and they just seem to get better year on year.

Rheum × hybridum 'Timperley Early'

Rhubarb 'Timperley Early'

Height 3ft (1m) **Spread** 6½ft (2m) **Time of flower** N/A **Soil** Moist but well-drained **Position** Full sun **Hardiness** Hardy

I have grown rhubarb since I was a kid, partly because I love to eat it, but also because it is so easy to grow, and I have happily interplanted it with ornamental plants for years. There are a lot of varieties to choose from, but 'Timperley Early' is a good starting place. I think it's one of the best early varieties—it's a hard-working plant that clumps well and has thick stems that are rich red at the base, fading toward the large, deep green, heart-shaped leaves. Rhubarb loves a sunny, well-drained spot but will deal with a little shade in a more neutral to slightly acidic soil—that said, it does fine in my limey soil. I add lots of organic matter and mulch every year, but never on top of the crown. If you have wetter soils, you need to improve the drainage. If newly planted, leave for a few years before pulling stems for the kitchen, from March onward. Once established it will force well, but I only do that every few years—cover the crown from January by using an overturned container or a terracotta planter (which make a great focal point). Forcing rhubarb produces sweet, tender stems—just keep an eye on them, as the slugs seem to enjoy them, too!

Ribes odoratum 'Dorothea's Early'

Buffalo currant

Height 3ft (1m) **Spread** 3ft (1m) **Time of flower** Spring **Soil** Well-drained **Position** Full sun/partial shade **Hardiness** Hardy

Ribes is a great group of shrubs, both edible and ornamental, deciduous and evergreen. I'm always on the lookout for something a little different, and this plant fits the bill! Known as the buffalo currant, its North American heritage makes it a tough little shrub, and I'm not sure why you don't see it more often. It carries wonderful clusters of yellow flowers in spring above rich green foliage, which have soft red throats and a sweet scent, followed by masses of dark black, tasty berries. It does not seem over-demanding soil-wise, but I do incorporate organic matter and mulch each year.

Rubus arcticus

Arctic bramble

Height 8in (20cm) **Spread** 12in (30cm) **Time of flower** Summer **Soil** Moist but well-drained **Position** Full sun/partial shade **Hardiness** Hardy

Raspberry, but not as you know it! I do love one of the common names of this plant, which is "Arctic raspberry." I just like the idea of walking across the Arctic and coming across raspberries! When I say this is a raspberry but not as you know it, it's because this little beauty only gets to around 8in (20cm). It makes a lovely groundcover and is tough and happy in the sun or partial shade in reasonable garden soil. It really is a great little addition and a nice surprise—I like using it between stepping stones. The plant is thornless and has small, bramble-like leaves that carry those same toothed margins. In late spring and early summer, dark pink, single flowers sit just above the foliage and pull in the bees. Flowers are followed by reddish fruits that seem to have a little flavor of the tropics, but the show does not stop there—come fall, the leaves turn a deep, rich red.

Rumex scutatus 'Silver Shield'

French sorrel

Height 20in (50cm) **Spread** 24in (60cm) **Time of flower** Summer **Soil** Moist but well-drained **Position** Full sun/partial shade **Hardiness** Hardy

Another beautiful edible herb, as the name suggests, it has silver, shield-shaped leaves with green veining that starts at the joint between leaf and stem. The plant grows in low, creeping, soft mounds, so it's good as groundcover at the front of a border or as relief in a busy bed. It's a tough plant that seems to put up with drought conditions, which can result in it taking on a reddish tone! It can get a little gangly in the season, but just take the hedge-trimmers across the top, and it soon comes back with lovely fresh growth—a bit like a cut-and-come-again lettuce. This *Rumex* is not really grown for its flowers, which are green, but they do come to the fore in fall when they turn to seed and darken. It's a great choice for cooks because the leaves have a good acidic kick and work really well with fish, soups, or a summer salad.

Rheum x hybridum 'Timperley Early'

Rubus arcticus

Ribes odoratum 'Dorothea's Early'

Rumex scutatus 'Silver Shield'

47

SOUTH-FACING WALL

I estimate I've got 14 different varieties of fruit trees in our south-facing, sunny front garden, including apples, pears, nectarines, greengages, damsons, and peaches—which seems like a lot for a small space. Essentially, I suppose it's a small orchard.

The choice of cultivar, the shape, and the placement of your fruit trees is important. I've got a nectarine growing on the front wall of the house along with a couple of pears and some climbing roses, and on a warm summer's day, the limestone walls seem to just suck up the heat. The spot isn't one you pass every day, so when I gave Mrs. Frost one

Light summer pruning of nectarine trees after fruiting.

of the first nectarines and she bit into it, and the wonderful juice ran down her chin, she said, "Wow, where did you get that from?" When I told her I'd grown it, she didn't believe me until I took her outside to show her the fruit growing on the tree. What did I say about memories?

Using any trained fruit is a great way of making your walls and boundaries work harder, and I also love the structural look it brings. However, there's an art to it. I fan the fruit across the wall in the same way that I train the fruit trees across the fence in the entrance (see page 23).

Part of growing fruit trees successfully is knowing where those cold winter winds might come from, looking out for late frosts, and making sure to drop a cover over for protection, if needed. Understanding the microclimates will mean you get more from the space. Basically, experience helps, but understanding your plot and your plants and knowing how to make them happy make all the difference. It's also about learning from your mistakes and things that fail, because they will at times—just don't worry about it. Pears and apples can handle harsher conditions than peaches and nectarines, which also love the heat radiated back from the stone wall, from which the fruit benefit.

Pruning

There's a lot of information out there about pruning trees, and while it can seem overwhelming, with time and practice, you will get a feel for it. For me, tailoring, controlling, and guiding is one of the arts of gardening. When to prune varies; in general, fruits such as stone fruit tend to be better off with a summer prune, as they heal quicker, which helps prevent bacterial infection, but don't worry too much if you break that rule. You can go out there with a pair of sharp pruners and spend a couple of hours tying things in and cutting things back, trimming away any dead, damaged, or diseased branches, and then when you stand back, it will give you a real sense of satisfaction. It's not as complicated as some of the books imply, and it is worth learning to do well, because your fruit trees will be more attractive, healthier, and more productive.

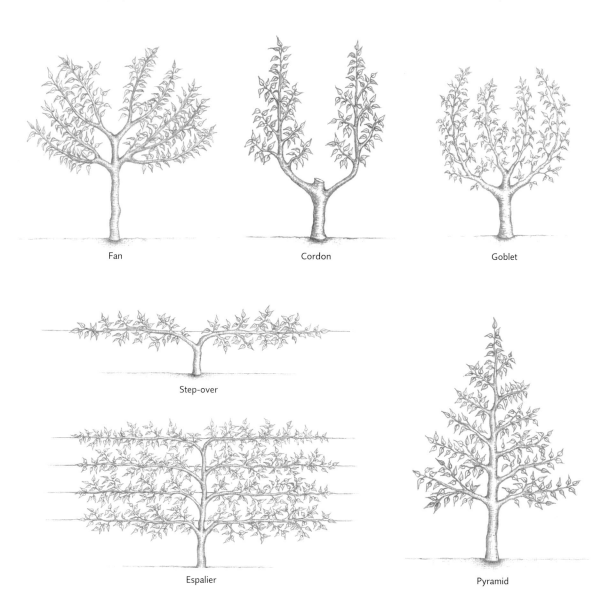

Fan

Cordon

Goblet

Step-over

Espalier

Pyramid

49

Gage 'Stella's Star'
Hector's greengage

Height 13ft (4m) **Spread** 13ft (4m) **Time of flower** Spring **Soil** Moist but well-drained **Position** Full sun/partial shade **Hardiness** Hardy

We had a gage and a damson in our garden when we were kids; they were big old standard trees, and I used to love climbing them and sitting up there, gorging on the fruit, usually after watching *Tarzan*! But you don't need a lot of room, as they can be grown as fans or espaliers, and they not only provide but look great too! This gage is named after the breeder's daughter, but you may also hear it called "Hector's." It's self-fertilizing, so you don't need other trees for pollination, and it starts producing fruit very early in its life. The pinky-white blossom gives way to fruits that look lovely as they ripen, turning soft pale yellow in late summer, and the flavor is subtle and lovely straight from the tree—great in puddings and jams! It prefers a sheltered spot with good light, good drainage, and soil prepped well with plenty of manure. I also like to feed and mulch annually.

Malus domestica 'Lord Burghley'
Apple 'Lord Burghley'

Height Varies **Spread** Varies **Time of flower** Spring **Soil** Moist but well-drained **Position** Full sun/partial shade **Hardiness** Hardy

This is a lovely way to add apples to your garden; think local, and you can find something that has been raised in your area. You will be surprised at how many apples are out there, for gardens of all sizes. This particular little beauty was raised at Burghley, in Stamford, Lincolnshire; it first fruited in 1834, then introduced in 1865. The tree is covered with pinky-white blossoms in spring, then the good-looking dessert apples ripen from midsummer to fall and last well into winter, which would have been very important at the time when it was introduced. Taste-wise, it is quite a fresh, sweet apple. I grow it as a step-over at the end of the vegetable garden.

Morus nigra
Black mulberry

Height 33–39ft (10–12m) **Spread** 26ft (8m) **Time of flower** Spring **Soil** Moist but well-drained **Position** Full sun **Hardiness** Hardy

King James offered 10,000 saplings to his lieutenants or cheap seeds to create plantations and kick off the English silk industry, which was worth a fortune. The only flaw in his plan was the black mulberry, as silkworms seem to prefer feeding on the white mulberry, which is native to China. I imagine someone lost their head over that! If you've ever eaten a mulberry fresh from the tree, I promise you will want to grow them. The white mulberry produces the most fruit, but I love the more common black mulberry. *Morus nigra* has a rugged feel to the bark and makes an architectural statement. That said, it's very versatile—I have seen it trained against a wall, grown as a multi-stem, pruned as a shrub, and even in a pot! If you grow it as a standard, give it room to spread. I enjoy the way the tree buds in spring with rich green, heart-shaped leaves and a pale underside that, come fall, turns a glorious yellow. The delicious, juicy mulberries ripen in late summer—just don't eat them while wearing a white T-shirt! You must be patient, as it takes a while to fruit.

Prunus persica var. *nectarina* 'Lord Napier'

Nectarine 'Lord Napier'

Height 10ft (3m) **Spread** 10ft (3m) **Time of flower** Spring **Soil** Moist but well-drained **Position** Full sun **Hardiness** Hardy (some protection from frost)

I can remember moving to Barnsdale and seeing a peach on a wall and thinking, "It looks nice, but it won't fruit." Well, they gave it a little winter protection, and yes, it did! Fast-forward 20-plus years, and I have a 'Lord Napier' fan tree on a south-facing wall that grows really well, producing large nectarines in mid- to late summer. I don't protect it in the winter, as it is sheltered from the cold and rain where it's planted, which helps prevent leaf curl. My house is constructed from limestone and really sucks up the heat, so no doubt that creates a little microclimate, too. The fruit ripens in August to a rich crimson color, and the flesh is very juicy, to the point that it's hard to stop it from running down your chin! Being self-fertilizing, it does not require another nectarine tree to pollinate the pretty pink spring flowers, but protection from frost when in bloom is essential.

Prunus 'Warwickshire Drooper'

Plum 'Warwickshire Drooper'

Height 8–13ft (2.5–4m) **Spread** 8–13ft (2.5–4m) **Time of flower** Spring **Soil** Moist but well-drained **Position** Full sun **Hardiness** Hardy

The name tells you a lot about this lovely old plum, which was bred in the 1920s in the West Midlands and has a cascading habit when in full fruit. It's a really good all-rounder; the fruit is great fresh from the tree, plus it works well in desserts and for a long time was grown commercially. You can see why, as it is a good performer. It is self-fertilizing, so it can be grown alone, which is a great start. You will find this plum available in different forms, which means it can work in varying-sized gardens. I grow it as a fan on a west-facing fence, but that said, it will take a little shade. The leaves are oval in shape and at times fold a little, and the tree is covered in white spring blossoms. This is followed by interesting oval, nearly egg-shaped fruit that has soft yellow skin and a reddish-brown finish and is ready for picking in late August/early September. It seems happy in most soils and does well in colder areas.

Pyrus communis 'Beurré Hardy'

Pear 'Beurré Hardy'

Height 13–26ft (4–8m) **Spread** 13–26ft (4–8m) **Time of flower** Spring **Soil** Moist but well-drained **Position** Full sun **Hardiness** Hardy

I have a few different pears in the garden, probably because I have a soft spot for the odd pear and blackberry cobbler. But if I had to choose one, it would be this French number that dates back to the early nineteenth century and has a great heritage! I have a couple of espalier trees in my front garden, as it is a great eater and has always been healthy and hard-working. It has strong leaves with a wonderful shine and a spring display of pure white flowers that seem to stand up well to late frosts. The fruits have a distinctive, aromatic rose-like smell and a flesh that's soft and sweeter than most pears, but I also really like the shape, which is more squat and rounded. As the fruit ripens, it turns from greenish-yellow to blushed green-red. The trees can be acquired in different forms, and as a standard, it can make a good statement tree. It needs a pollination partner pear and pairs well with 'Doyenne du Comice', which I also grow. I mulch my trees well and provide a spring feed.

COURTYARD

"Secret Garden"—Bruce Springsteen

To get to this part of the garden you have to open a gate, and it really does feel like a "Secret Garden." The space draws you in and holds you with its simplicity; there is a gentle calmness about it.

Shapes, forms, textures, and wonderful shades of green. Green creates calmness.

The front door to the house is actually around the side, which I think is more interesting and provides me with a great opportunity to do something a little different with the approach. So, the first thing to do was to enclose that space and break up the movement through it. Rather than simply letting visitors walk straight up to the front door, I've introduced a nicely crafted wood gate and fence as a sort of pausing point before entering the shady courtyard tucked between our house and the neighbors.

I think of this courtyard as a garden's version of a palate cleanser. You leave the sunny front garden to enter a partly shaded area before reaching the front door. The courtyard area measures 23–26ft (7–8m) long and 10–13ft (3–4m) wide, and although it's the size of a small garden, when we moved in, there was very little of interest other than some climbing hydrangea (*Hydrangea petiolaris*) on the fence, so you tended to walk straight past it and through the space. The hydrangea had been neglected and become a little unruly, but instead of pruning back to the fence, I added a few stakes to support parts of the plant, then encouraged other stems to embrace the main structural planting provided by tree ferns. This really set the tone for the area as you transition from space to space.

The ferns come as a real surprise as you leave the warmth and lightness of the meadow, herbs, and edibles and come through the gate to be met with deep shade, luscious green planting, and a reliance on form and foliage rather than flowers. I'd say it's the biggest surprise in the whole garden. The overall effect of this greenery is that the garden instantly looks and feels cooler and carries a calmer atmosphere, and you do feel as if you have found something; the idea of a more secret place, maybe prehistoric. The first time I saw tree ferns en masse was at the Lost Gardens of Heligan, in Cornwall: I walked down the bottom of the steep-sided valley to a lush, exotic-looking area filled with subtropical tree ferns, and I was blown away. I seriously love tree ferns, and the fact that they've been growing on the planet since prehistoric times is just incredible. I mean, how does anything survive that long?

For some reason, this courtyard never gets frost. I suspect it's because it sits between two limestone houses, and next door gets some east-facing sun, and my side gets a bit of west-facing sun. So, I think there's a little microclimate going on. It also sits lower than the back garden and has a hedge boundary to the north, so the wind is filtered. We get a little southwesterly wind, but it doesn't tend to be cold.

FERNS AND WOODLAND PLANTS

The courtyard seemed the perfect space for the tree ferns, so I worked in as many as I could, and a couple of them are a fair height, so you see them as you walk through the front garden. Then, as you pass through the gate, you have to engage with the ferns, some of which encroach onto the path, breaking the straight line.

Rather than plant all the ferns in a uniform manner, I set them at different angles. You literally have to duck under the fronds of the tree ferns to enter the courtyard, which probably annoys everyone a little bit, but I really enjoy creating this sort of physical engagement with a space. The little courtyard sits in isolation, so there's even more of a wow factor and feeling of secrecy when you're in it. This planting also means visitors are obliged to slow down and hopefully take a bit of time to appreciate it all—the underside of the fronds are well worth a look. Just outside the front door, there's a spot where you can sit down and take a moment while you put your boots on.

I did a similar thing for a show garden at the 2015 RHS Chelsea Flower Show. I planted bright colors in front of a huge, modern garden room, but tucked away behind it was a small enclosed space that I planted with tree ferns. So, when you sat in the building, you could turn around and look into something lush, green, and completely different than the strong orange and crimson colors you

saw when you first walked in. Often, tiny little ideas like that bumble around in my head until I find the opportunity to make them reality. In fact, the tree ferns I used here were actually from that 2015 garden.

Gardens are driven by atmospheres, from hot to cool, from strong to soft, and the rest of the planting here relies on various shades of green, so it's all about foliage, texture, form, and finish. I've a particularly good oak-leaved hydrangea called *Hydrangea quercifolia* 'Queen of Hearts' and a lovely Solomon's seal called *Polygonatum odoratum* 'Flatmate', which is unusual in that it has red stems that look as if they have been pressed flat. Essentially, I wanted some really interesting bits to catch your eye and draw you in as you start looking down on it.

The thing is, I really love woodland plants, so I began researching and collecting a mix for this spot. Some are really quite unusual, such as *Syneilesis subglabrata*, wild ginger (*Saruma henryi*), and *Chloranthus japonicus*. Even the bulb planting in this area is quite subtle, using *Erythronium revolutum* and *Camassia leichtlinii* 'Blue Heaven'.

Encouraging the *Hydrangea petiolaris* to wrap round the tree ferns and tying it onto the wooden stake as a support.

Planting Plan

Trees and Shrubs

- *Dicksonia antarctica*
- *Hydrangea petiolaris*
- *Hydrangea quercifolia* 'Queen of Hearts'

Perennials

- *Bergenia ciliata* 'Wilton'
- *Chloranthus fortunei* 'Domino'

- *Disporopsis fuscopicta*
- *Epimedium* 'Spine Tingler'
- *Hakonechloa macra*
- *Polygonatum odoratum* 'Flatmate'
- *Polystichum neolobatum*
- *Dryopteris championii*
- *Saruma henryi*
- *Syneilesis subglabrata*

Drifts

Erythronium revolutum

Camassia leichtlinii 'Blue Heaven'

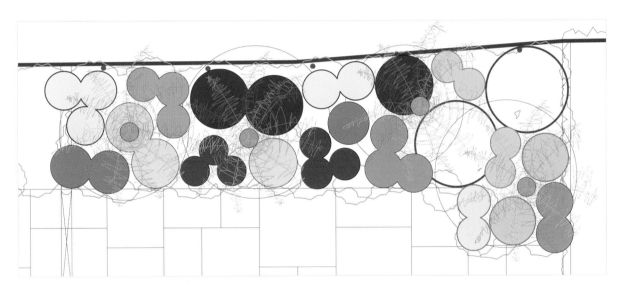

Shade-loving pots also provide some focal interest worked through the space. There's a mixture of hostas, more ferns, epimediums, and impatiens.

At the end of the courtyard, I planted a large container with a dark-leaved Japanese maple called *Acer palmatum* 'Bloodgood', which provides a focal point, and the red-purple leaves against the rich-green leaves of the hornbeam hedge look stunning. It's the only dark element

here. It also ties the space to the back garden, where there's another acer.

The courtyard is partly wrapped by a hornbeam hedge that continues round the corner to the lower terrace, dividing the space from the rear garden. The hedge is underplanted with wild garlic, as the paving around it means the herb won't spread uncontrollably.

From left to right:
Hydrangea quercifolia,
Syneilesis subglabrata,
and *Dicksonia antarctica.*

Bergenia ciliata 'Wilton'

Elephant's ears 'Wilton'

Height 12in (30cm) **Spread** 18in (45cm) **Time of flower** Late spring **Soil** Good, moist, humus-rich **Position** Dappled shade/partial shade **Hardiness** Fully hardy

I think lots of us know elephant's ears from our grandparents' gardens. This variety is not one of those! First, the *ciliata* varieties are all deciduous, so they lose their leaves in winter, which I think makes it even more lovely when it flowers with pink blooms in spring. The stem sits well above newly forming foliage, leaves that are quite small to start but can end up the size of dinner plates, with a matte, textured finish. These leaves carry hundreds of small hairs, so the whole thing feels soft. As the plant grows, the undersides of the leaves are a pinky-gray color and provide a charming contrast with the top sides. I did have some of these plants in pots to start with, but one got scorched by a little too much sun, so they really do like a shady spot. I also mulch mine really well with well-rotted manure, which not only helps feed the plant but also is good for moisture retention. These plants can look quite lovely in the early morning light.

Chloranthus japonicus

Japanese chloranthus

Height 12in (30cm) **Spread** 8in (20cm) **Time of flower** Spring **Soil** Moist but well-drained **Position** Full sun/partial shade **Hardiness** Fully hardy

This is a plant I first bought about 10 years ago, and for the first few years, I played around with growing it in pots. Originally from Japan, it has been around for a long time and is quite an unusual perennial. You don't see it all over; in the wild, it grows in forests and alongside streams. To start with, I could not get it to flower regularly in pots, but as soon as I put it in the garden, in shade and a good rich soil, it was a lot happier and is now flowering well. It seems to be a plant that benefits from just being given a bit more time. It is a fascinating little plant; the rootstock clumps up slowly as it emerges in the spring, pushing up stems that are a reddish color, topped with four leaves that sit at the quarter angle. The leaves are oval with a serrated edge and a glossy finish, above which sits a small, white, bottle-brush-shaped flower. It looks great coming up through lower planting or interplanted with ferns.

Dicksonia antarctica

Soft tree fern

Height 10ft (3m) **Spread** 6½ft (2m) **Time of flower** N/A **Soil** Well-drained **Position** Partial shade/full shade **Hardiness** Hardy (protect from frost in colder areas)

It doesn't seem that long ago when these plants were only really associated with the southwest of Britain, but now they are all over the country—and you can see why. For me, they are of a different world, carrying an atmosphere all their own. It's hard to comprehend that these plants predate dinosaurs! When it comes to planting, if I can, I use a few, as they do look great grouped. I know, that sounds a little extravagant, but sometimes I just can't help myself, and they are a wonderful surprise as you walk through my side gate. I find it truly fascinating to watch the crosiers unfurl, which just keep coming from spring right through to midsummer. They seem to be the most reliable tree fern to grow in the UK. I have planted them in a humus-rich soil in an area that is partly shaded and sheltered from cold winds, which can be a problem for these plants. I protect the crown of the trunk in the winter by trimming the fronds and turning them back in over the crown. Then, come spring, as new crosiers begin to form, I cover the trunks with fleece. The crowns are quite something, but I also love the trunks; they just ooze history and are really tactile, but they're also covered in aerial roots, which means you could cut through the trunk and put the top into the ground, and it would root (I am not saying do it!).

Disporopsis fuscopicta

Height 20in (50cm) **Spread** 20in (50cm) **Time of flower** Late spring **Soil** Good, moist, humus-rich **Position** Partial shade/full shade **Hardiness** Fully hardy

A relative of the Solomon's seal family, this variety starts to cover ground with interesting rhizomes that scrabble about, and from these grow arching stems that are a lovely purple color at the bottom, fading to green farther up. The stems vary in height on each plant, which creates layering, like a mini woodland. The leaves are evergreen and have a shiny finish, then in late spring, small, white, bell-shaped flowers hang from the stems, washed with the same purple color in the inside and tips of the flowers. The blooms carry a little fragrance, which is a wonderful surprise, and then dark berries can follow in fall, but that has been a little hit or miss for me. In my experience, it did take a while to get going, but in year 2, it really got its roots in, and off it went!

Bergenia ciliata 'Wilton'

Dicksonia antarctica

Chloranthus japonicus

Disporopsis fuscopicta

Epimedium 'Spine Tingler'
Barrenwort

Height 12in (30cm) **Spread** 12in (30cm) **Time of flower** Spring **Soil** Well-drained **Position** Sun/partial shade **Hardiness** Fully hardy

I love the name of this plant—it should be the title of a song! I think it's fantastic. It has very distinctive leaves that are serrated and have a glossy finish; when they first emerge, they are bronze flushed with pink, slowly deepening in color to tones of greens and browns. I find the leaves quite quickly clump up, and the plant can become covered in soft, yellow, spider-like flowers. The interesting thing with this plant is that the blooms arrive at the same time as the foliage, which makes it different from other epimediums. I would grow this just for its foliage, so the flowers really are a bonus! It does seem to like a good humus-rich soil that will retain a little moisture, so I plant it in partial and full shade, in particular under shrubs and small trees. I don't cut off the old foliage until I see the new foliage just starting to emerge.

Dryopteris championii
Champion's wood fern

Height 24in (60cm) **Spread** 20in (50cm) **Time of flower** N/A **Soil** Moist, well-drained, tolerates drier soils **Position** Dappled shade/partial shade **Hardiness** Fully hardy

I really love the texture and finishes of ferns and enjoy creating tapestries with them. This is a really useful evergreen fern that I think is underused. It seems tough and clumps slowly but well, and the fronds are a rich green with a satin finish, stand upright, and last well through the winter. The stems carry reddish scales, which are a lovely contrast to the textured foliage. The new growth emerges a little later in the spring than some other ferns, and the crosiers are covered in small, lightly colored hairs. That late arrival is great if your garden is prone to late frost. The foliage color deepens over the season and looks wonderful in winter.

Erythronium revolutum

Erythronium revolutum
Mahogany fawn lily

Height 12in (30cm) **Spread** 4in (10cm) **Time of flower** Spring **Soil** Moist but well-drained **Position** Partial shade **Hardiness** Fully hardy

I have really gotten into these plants in the last few years. They seemed a little fleeting to me at one point, but it's funny how things change! That short time of flowering is pure joy. I can find myself losing time looking for their little stems early in the year, and that in itself is wonderful.

These dainty plants are like jewels of enjoyment, and I have a few worked through the area. Most erythroniums flower in early spring and then go back into the earth to chill out until the following spring. The leaves are green and mottled with a thin, wire-like stem that elegantly curves at the top and carries a soft-pink, lily-type flower that also curls back, seemingly inviting pollinators. It is really good in woodland, and it also seems to like the dry winter conditions of my garden.

Hakonechloa macra

Japanese forest grass

Height 16in (40cm) **Spread** 20in (50cm) **Time of flower** Summer **Soil** Moist but well-drained **Position** Partial shade/full shade **Hardiness** Fully hardy

This has become a bit of a go-to for designers, and you can see why, as it produces delicate arching leaves that come alive with a gust of wind, with a sound that just adds to its grace. It is known as Japanese forest grass, which I think tells you where it works best. Its star quality is as a wonderful foil for surrounding plants, proving that not all plants need to be stars in their own right! It has slender, bladed leaves that are paper-like and what I call a "healthy" green. Wispy green flowers arrive in late summer, which slowly deepen in color as the season moves on. In fall, leaves turn red-orange and then a softer brown, remaining over winter, so I don't cut them back until the new growth arrives. It works well in partial shade or shade and once established, it will handle drier conditions, although I do mulch the soil well. It can take a while to get going, but it's a very long-living plant.

Hydrangea petiolaris

Climbing hydrangea

Height 39ft+ (12m+) **Spread** 26ft (8m) **Time of flower** Summer **Soil** Moist, well-drained and fertile **Position** Full sun/partial shade/full shade **Hardiness** Fully hardy

I have always loved this hydrangea. It is a good worker—it just needs a bit of TLC to get it going and well established. I tend to make sure I'm planting it in well-composted soil to give it the best start. It really is a good choice for a north-facing wall. It's also an excellent reminder that not every climber needs to be evergreen, as this plant has great fall color—rich golden-yellow leaves—and when these fall, the bark peels to create an incredibly sculptural effect. And that's all after the arrival of large, white flowers in early summer, working well as a contrast to the dark green foliage. It really does pop in a shady spot.

Hakonechloa macra

Hydrangea petiolaris

Hydrangea quercifolia **'Queen of Hearts'**

Hydrangea 'Queen of Hearts'

Height 6½ft (2m) **Spread** 5–6½ft (1.5–2m) **Time of flower** Summer **Soil** Moist but well-drained **Position** Full sun/partial shade/full shade **Hardiness** Fully hardy

By the time I left the North Devon Parks Department, I would have been quite happy not to see a hydrangea again! We had them all over the place, and we used them for all the festivals, so plants would be stripped throughout festival season. Anyway, about 10 years ago, one of my friends asked, "Have you tried this hydrangea?" So I did, and guess what? I'm back into hydrangeas. Probably my favorites are the *quercifolia* types, whose oak-leaf-shaped leaves are a wonderful texture. 'Queen of Hearts' has a rounded but also quite free and easy growth habit of stems that are sandy brown with bark that peels in places. Cone-like white flowers protrude from the foliage, and later in summer these turn a rich pink, giving the plant a whole new layer of interest. In fall, the leaves turn a rich deep red, and then in winter, the tan-colored stems really come into their own. I tend to use these plants in partial or full shade, but they will do fine in the sun in a good rich soil, too. Another *quercifolia* I love is 'Ruby Slippers', which was selected at the same time as 'Queen of Hearts'.

Polygonatum odoratum 'Flatmate'
Solomon's Seal

Height 3ft (1m) **Spread** 20in (50cm) **Time of flower** Spring–summer **Soil** Moist but well-drained **Position** Partial shade/full shade **Hardiness** Fully hardy

Polygonatum are herbaceous perennials with erect or arching stems adorned with bell- or tubular-shaped flowers, followed by black or red berries. It's a plant my nan used to have, and I suppose to some, it is a little old-fashioned. Over the years, I have dropped in and out of playing with different varieties as they catch my eye, and in all honesty, they have been a little hit and miss, but the more unusual ones have worked—perhaps because I have paid them more attention! When it comes to a being little different, *Polygonatum odoratum* 'Flatmate' fits the bill. One of the larger varieties, it's the stems that are most impressive, flattened, as if pressed. The color of the stems can vary depending on light levels. The leaves are 4in (10cm) plus, with a sheen to the surface and a pale underside. The cream flowers have a green tip and hang under the stems as they start to arch. It seems happy in partial or full shade—I plant mine in woodland soil, which suits its rhizomatous root system.

Polystichum polyblepharum
Japanese lace fern

Height 20in (50cm) **Spread** 35in (90cm) **Time of flower** N/A **Soil** Well-drained **Position** Partial shade/full shade **Hardiness** Fully hardy

This is a beauty. Its fronds have a bright sheen that glows in the spring sun, and it looks lovely after a rain shower. One of this fern's strong points is it nearly always looks good, even early in the season, because the new fronds emerge covered in sandy golden hairs. The effect is stunning. It's a fern with wonderful texture; if you see it on a frosty morning, it will stop you in your tracks. It seems to favor a dappled shady site where the soil does not get too dry, but that said, it does not seem to like it very wet in winter. I have planted this in well-mulched soil in my garden, in quite a cool spot, which really plays to its strengths. It is great to experiment with in the garden, and I like to use it under and around strong forms.

Saruma henryi
Upright wild ginger

Height 18in (45cm) **Spread** 20in (50cm) **Time of flower** Spring **Soil** Rich, humusy, moist but well-drained **Position** Part shade/full shade **Hardiness** Fully hardy

This is a reasonably new plant for me, and I've only been growing it for a few years. I don't think it's been available that long. This is another "you need to try this" plant—a "wow, it is a little grafter!" *Saruma henryi* originates from China and is related to wild ginger. It is what's known as a monotypic plant, which means there is only one species in the genus—which fascinates me! It seems to be a really happy little woodlander. The leaves are heart-shaped and feel quite soft to the touch, set along stems that are like bronzed hairy legs—if a little gangly. I find it really easy to grow in moist but well-draining soil. In my garden, it flowers in later spring, producing yellow blooms that are slightly crimped but soft on the eye.

Syneilesis subglabrata
Palmate umbrella plant

Height 35in (90cm) **Spread** 8in (20cm)
Time of flower Summer–late summer **Soil**
Moist but well-drained **Position** Partial
shade/full shade **Hardiness** Fully hardy

This is a plant I bought from a friend a few
years ago, and it soon became one of my
favorites. I could not believe it was a
member of the daisy family when I first
discovered that. It is a beauty, and it has
really performed! I grow it under the tree
ferns, where the bold leaf is perfect against
the softer texture of the fern fronds. The
leaves make a real statement, appearing
umbrella-like—well, like one that has been
perfectly ripped by the wind. The stem
hits the leaf centrally, which drives that
umbrella feel, and it is eye-catching from
the moment it comes out of the ground.
The leaves carry a soft film to start with,
opening to a deep green. The white
flowers arrive in small clusters and are
nice enough, but that's not its draw! This
plant is good for a dry site. Another just as
lovely variety, but one that's not easy to get
hold of, is *Syneilesis aconitifolia*.

LOWER TERRACE

"Lucky Man"—Richard Ashcroft

This terrace is the first connection with the back of the house, the place where I enter the garden every day—normally with a cup of coffee in hand and accompanied by Ash and Islay. I feel like a "Lucky Man," and that feeling never seems to die.

Along the rear of the house runs the lower terrace, where I've created a mix of borders and a seating area where we can eat outside as a family. There are two points of entry to this space: from the back of the house or via the front door and courtyard at the side of the house.

Designing a garden is not just about beauty; it's about controlling how you move through a space. This is often achieved with walls, fences, hedges, and paths, but it can also be done with varying shapes and sizes of borders. I want to stop people in their tracks as they leave the courtyard and then guide them to the left of it in the direction of the main garden, where another view opens up.

This north border is, as you might guess, north-facing, and it can be viewed from three sides, with the house as the backdrop. A kitchen window looks straight out onto this border, so I wanted to use it to create a good view from inside the house, too. The back garden is split across three key levels: the lower terrace, main terrace, and upper terrace. A key part of my design thinking was "What views do I want to create at each level?" So, for the lower terrace, I had to imagine standing or sitting up on the main terrace, looking back down toward the house: What would I see? This is where the north border comes to the fore.

Rosa 'Shropshire Lass' popping up and pushing its way through the flowers of the *Ranunculus.*

THE NORTH BORDER

As you go up to the higher terraces of the rear garden and look back toward the house, the lower terrace, which is the lowest point, appears a bit like the bottom of a canyon. Adding a big deep bed near the house helps balance that space, adding height as well as depth.

The north border is about 10ft (3m) square. It is edged on three sides with York stone paving and blocks, which are textured and light in color. As well as helping guide people around the garden, because it's quite a deep bed, the north border visually helps bring the back wall of the cottage down into the garden. It forms a link between the garden and the house as well as between the lower and upper terraces. The wall is covered with climbing roses, which helps soften the house.

Importantly, the bed leads you from the predominantly green, nutty, over-the-top Heligan-esque aesthetic of the courtyard into the main plants of the garden. This bed also serves to filter the views and create some lovely little vignettes. In many ways, it's a transition border rather than a jump-in-your-face border, so I've designed it to be really easy on the eye, with a more classic mix of shrubs and herbaceous plants. It's got a feeling of calm about it.

Being a decent size, the bed also gave me an opportunity to put in a lovely little multi-stem tree, an *Amelanchier lamarckii*, about 10ft (3m) away from the house, which I've maintained with a dome-line top. It acts as a pivot point for the rest of the plants. Once the amelanchier was in, I added two strong yew domes, which bring a lovely visual connection to various other yew forms and a sort of movement through the garden.

I grow all my hostas in containers. I add a little nylon mesh at the bottom of the pot before filling it with potting mix. Someone at *Gardeners' World* suggested it, and it works!

Planting Plan

Trees and Shrubs

● *Amelanchier x lamarckii*

● *Rosa* 'Madame Alfred Carrière'

◯ *Rosa* 'Shropshire Lass'

● *Taxus baccata* (dome)

Perennials

Astrantia major 'Star of Billion'

● *Disporopsis fuscopicta*

Disporum longistylum

Disporum megalanthum

Epimedium 'Spine Tingler'

● *Geranium phaeum* 'Springtime'

● *Melica uniflora albida*

Paeonia daurica subsp. *mlokosewitschii*

● *Podophyllum* 'Spotty Dotty'

● *Sarcococca taiwaniana*

Bulbs

Galanthus nivalis

Camassia leichtlinii 'Sacajawea'

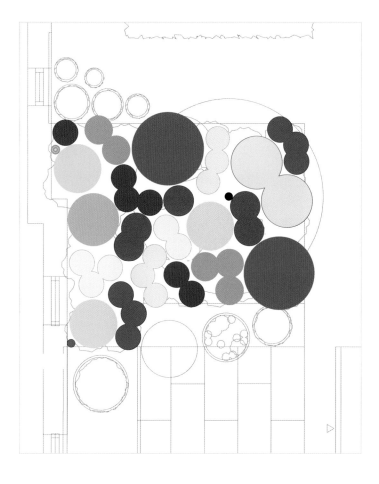

Although there's still a lot of green in the north border, I have introduced some color, too, from ornamental grasses such as *Melica altissima* 'Alba', along with geraniums, epimediums, disporums, disporopsis, and white astrantias, as well a few plants with variegated leaves. There's a lovely couple of Molly the witch peonies (*Paeonia mlokosewitschii*), which have pale lemon-yellow flowers in mid-spring. I've also started to introduce a few slightly darker colors, with plants like *Geranium phaeum* 'Springtime' and *Podophyllum* 'Spotty Dotty' all having dark elements to their foliage. In this way, I can connect them with the amelanchier, and this helps change the mood of the space. In terms of the bulb layer, I've put in some snowdrops and variegated camassias. The lower terrace is also where I use a lot of my shade-loving pots, such as hostas.

When clipping *Taxus* domes, I put down fleece before I start, which collects the trimmings and helps with the cleanup!

Astrantia major 'Star of Billion'

Masterwort, Hattie's pincushion

Height 31–35in (80–90cm) **Spread** 20in (50cm) **Time of flower** Summer **Soil** Most types **Position** Full sun/partial shade **Hardiness** Fully hardy

I think it was Geoff Hamilton who introduced me to astrantias. They are a bit of a cottage garden favorite, but, that said, they do work in so many styles, which means they have been a good go-to for me ever since. I don't think I create a garden now that does not have one or two astrantias in it, as they are just great-value perennials. 'Star of Billion' has mid-green, deeply cut leaves that have a satin finish, so they work well with softer foliages. The white flowers arrive in good numbers: little pincushions surrounded with white bracts that carry a green tip. It will flower for a good portion of the summer—mine even tend to have a second flush, and although this is not as prolific, I do love the contrast with the earlier flowers. Happy in most soils, I find the more they are in the sun, the more they need moisture. Once they get going, they settle in nicely and offer up great cut flowers for the house that last a long time in water.

Disporum longistylum

Long-styled disporum

Height 3–5ft (90–150cm) **Spread** 12in (30cm) **Time of flower** Late spring–early summer **Soil** Rich and fertile **Position** Partial shade/shade **Hardiness** Fully hardy

Although this plant is a member of the Solomon's seal family, *Disporum longistylum* does not come with some of the problems to which its family members are susceptible. The stems of the plant are bamboo-like and a rich deep purple to start, changing to a dark green, arching toward the tips. The plant carries soft clusters of dainty, green to cream, bell-shaped flowers that are followed by deep purple-black berries. I tend to leave the old stems standing into winter, not only to provide interest in the garden but to support the new growth the following year. It loves a nice humus-rich soil in shade to semi-shade and is a really classy woodlander that I like to plant with lower textural plants, as this helps highlight its elegance. This group of plants will show some variations when grown from seed.

Disporum megalanthum

Fairy bells

Height 20–24in (50–60cm) **Spread** 20in (50cm) **Time of flower** Spring **Soil** Rich and fertile **Position** Partial shade/shade **Hardiness** Fully hardy

If, like me, you have fallen for *Disporum* but want something a little shorter, this could be the one for you. Its leaves are a lovely deep green with a glossy finish and are slightly more rounded than *Disporum longistylum*. The flowers—creamy white bells that hang in clusters on arching stems—are larger than those of other *Disporum* species, and they really do catch the eye. You need to see them in a soft breeze, when they show off their wonderful nodding heads. The flowers are followed by dark red berries that carry you into fall. It's a good woodlander that loves a cool, rich soil—mine sits near a north-facing wall and is quite happy there.

Galanthus nivalis
Common snowdrop

Height 4in (10cm) **Spread** 4in (10cm) **Time of flower**
Late winter–early spring **Soil** Moderately fertile, moist,
well-drained **Position** Full sun/partial shade **Hardiness**
Fully hardy

Is there a better bulb than a snowdrop? I'm not one who
needs to find every variety going, but I do look forward to
the yearly show from a group of snowdrops in my garden.
There is a purity about it, and it signals that we are on the
move with our seasons. For me, they are quite reliable,
blooming as early as January and February. We know and
love them for their small, white, bell-shaped flowers,
although there is now a mind-blowing range of sizes,
colors, markings, and numbers of petal shapes. Some
varieties will set you back a good amount of money, but I
like to keep it simple. Most people like to plant snowdrops
in the green in February and March, but to save money,
I tend to buy the bulbs in late summer, grow them in
containers, then plant them out the following spring. This
is not just a lot cheaper; the success rate is also better
than planting straight into the ground, as I can control the
conditions over winter. After a few years, I normally dig up
and divide any plants that are looking a little congested.

Galanthus nivalis

Geranium phaeum 'Springtime'

Geranium phaeum 'Springtime'
Dusky cranesbill

Height 16–20in (40–50cm) **Spread** 16–20in (40–50cm)
Time of flower Late spring–early summer **Soil** Rich but
well-drained **Position** Full sun/full shade/partial shade
Hardiness Fully hardy

Phaeum geraniums have become a bit of go-to for
me; they are what I call one of my old friends, as
you can normally find one to suit any spot. This one
is a little different; I don't always take to variegation,
but every now and again, something catches my eye.
With 'Springtime', it's the way the leaf evolves as the
season moves on, because the new foliage emerges
creamy white in the center, with green edges. As the
temperatures rise, the leaves gradually turn a mid-green,
with deeper maroon markings. The deep-purple flowers
have crinkly-edged petals and pick up beautifully on the
dark markings of the leaf. As I said, it's a good worker,
but it does need to be rewarded with a good moisture-
retentive soil. Although it grows best in shade, it can
work well enough in partial sun.

Melica uniflora f. albida
Wood melick

Height 12–16in (30–40cm) **Spread** 24in (60cm) **Time of flower** Spring–early summer **Soil** Most types **Position** Full sun/partial shade **Hardiness** Fully hardy

This little grass is full of grace, and the one thing it has over *Hakonechloa macra* is its little white flowers, which look like tiny grains of rice and arrive in later spring and early summer, when it really comes into its own. I personally don't find it as reliable as *Hakonechloa,* but that does not stop me growing it, which tells you something! It is wonderful for a shady spot. I like to use it in and around stronger forms, as it provides a softening touch and works well with many other plants. The sprays of flowers bring a lovely airiness to borders, and it's especially useful for brightening up shady spots. It doesn't need a lot of care—I have it planted in a good well-mulched soil where I'd improved the drainage by adding a little sand—and when it comes to maintenance, I cut it back in early spring before new foliage emerges. It will colonize the ground over time, but if it outgrows the space, simply dig up and divide the plants in early spring.

Paeonia daurica subsp. *mlokosewitschii*

Paeonia daurica subsp. mlokosewitschii
Mlokosewitch's peony

Height 31in (80cm) **Spread** 20in (50cm) **Time of flower** Spring **Soil** Rich and fertile **Position** Full sun/partial shade **Hardiness** Fully hardy

Many people think peonies are a flash in the pan, but I don't fall into that camp. A peony in full flower is glorious, however long it lasts, and if you are a fan, this one will soon be on your radar. Yes, the name is a mouthful, so most call it "Molly the Witch." There is something unique about the perfect bowls of cool, lemon-yellow single flowers that look like a hedgehog of golden stamens and purple stigmas. It is a clump-forming herbaceous perennial, with flowers that arrive earlier than many peonies, usually in April. Mine are planted on the corner of a border that I pass every day. From the moment it breaks ground, early buds and young leaves are a rich pink-flushed bronze, maturing to soft, glaucous, bluish-green leaves. The flower buds seem to last forever, which just helps build the anticipation. Don't plant them too deep, or they may struggle to flower. You might want to be seated when you look at the price of these plants—mine were a birthday present from Mrs. Frost! They are expensive because they can be quite hard to get hold of.

Melica uniflora f. *albida*

Podophyllum versipelle 'Spotty Dotty'

Mayapple 'Spotty Dotty'

Height 12–16in (30–40cm) **Spread** 16–20in (40–50cm)
Time of flower Late spring–early summer **Soil** Moist, but
well-drained **Position** Partial shade/full shade **Hardiness**
Fully hardy

This is definitely a "Marmite" plant, and it's one of my
oldest daughter's favorites. The first time I saw it, I was
not sure how to use it, but I think its oddity really grew on
me. Initially, I grew this in pots and kept moving it around
until I found things it worked with. Over time, I have used
it in different ways; I particularly love it as a complete
contrast, working it into a sea of green fern. It does pick
up well with the *Geranium phaeum* 'Springtime' (see
page 78) and can help move the eye. 'Spotty Dotty' is
a hybrid *Podophyllum*, related to the North American
species *Podophyllum peltatum*. It is happy in a moisture-
retentive soil in shade, and it provides a little drama from
early in the season. As new growth emerges, it pushes
up through the soil like a small closed umbrella, then
opens once it clears the soil surface and clumps over
time. Interestingly, all the leaves seem to differ a little;
the markings on this plant are fascinating, starting really
brightly and fading. As the season moves on, there is a
mix of greens with brown to bronze blotches. In late
spring and early summer, it produces long, pendulous,
bell-shaped, crimson flowers that hang beneath the
leaves.

Podophyllum versipelle 'Spotty Dotty'

Sarcococca taiwaniana
Winter box

Height 20–24in (50–60cm) **Spread** 20in (50cm) **Time of flower** Winter–early spring **Soil** Rich, but well-drained **Position** Partial shade/shade **Hardiness** Fully hardy

Sarcococca hookeriana and S. *confusa* are widely available, reliable plants, and I have always liked them, so when I came across S. *taiwaniana* a few years ago, it really piqued my interest. It's a winner, with a slightly sprawling, suckering habit, and yet it is still compact—if that makes sense! Stems are dark green and elliptical in shape, and this little shrub seems to freely produce white, dented flowers with a fabulous scent, followed by small purple-black berries. Easily grown in shade to light shade in a humus-rich soil that is reasonably drained, I have it happily tucked against a north-facing wall, but I have also used it as hedging.

Taxus baccata
Common yew

Height 39ft+ (12m+) **Spread** 26ft+ (8m+) **Time of flower** N/A **Soil** Moist but well-drained **Position** Full sun/dappled shade/full shade **Hardiness** Fully hardy

This British native, evergreen tree has been traditionally used for hedging and topiary. It is incredibly long-lived and has a great history—there are two in my local churchyard, and I do wonder sometimes what they have seen! A yew brings great presence to any garden and works well for classic or modern styles. I enjoy using it to punch it through a border, even into a lawn, to draw the eye and provide great form and a deep rich green as a background for other plants. The small leaves will withstand hard clipping, and unlike conifers, if you inherit an overgrown plant, you can regenerate it by cutting hard back to the main trunk or even stump. Yew will grow in most soils, but it does need to be well-drained, as it does not like its roots wet for too long! Happy in sun or shade, we do forget sometimes that these clipped forms provide great habitat for birds and other wildlife. I grow mine as domes, which I trim twice annually to maintain a good, neat shape.

Sarcococca taiwaniana

Taxus baccata

MAIN TERRACE

"Mr. Brightside"—The Killers

This is really the family part of the garden, so they chose the song here! It needed to be one that got them all dancing, from the youngest to the oldest, and that is "Mr. Brightside." There is a freedom about the planting in this part of the garden; it feels full of life.

Following the steps up from the lower terrace, you reach the main terrace, which is about 3ft (90cm) higher and encompasses a good diversity of planting, including a mixed-species lawn. This is an area where people can wander, sit, cook, and take a breath—it's the area we use a lot as a family.

When we moved in, you looked directly onto this part of the garden from the house, but it didn't really feel right, as you could see too far without anything dividing the space. Although I didn't want the whole garden revealed at once, I also didn't want to block the view too much. So, it was really about balance and letting the plants define the area. There is now a retaining wall in front of the main terrace, with a 5ft (1.4m) deep bed behind it, which means that the view across the main

This cross-section (right) of the back garden shows the layout from the lower terrace up to the upper terrace, over five levels and 8ft (2.5m). The overhead photo below shows a section across the width of the garden and the steps linking the various terraces.

North border in the lower terrace

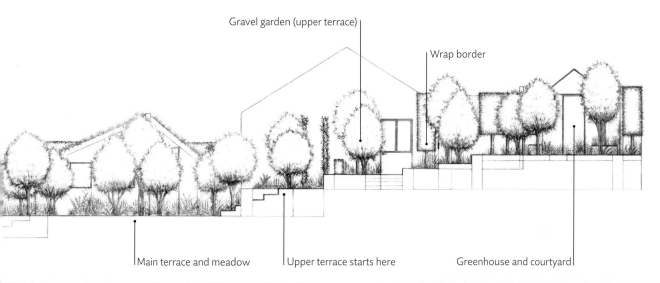

Gravel garden (upper terrace)

Wrap border

Main terrace and meadow

Upper terrace starts here

Greenhouse and courtyard

terrrace is interupted by a large mass of undulating plants at eye level as you walk along the lower terrace.

Although separate areas, I still wanted to keep a connection between them. To do this, I made the steps of the central staircase that rise to the main terrace over 6½ft (2m) wide. As well as tying the two areas together visually, this gives me enough space to arrange pots on the steps.

The main terrace makes the most of the widest part of the garden. It's a large rectangular area that wraps around a mixed-species lawn. I have placed focal points at either end so you've got nice views in both directions, and you can choose either to go to the left or turn right at the top of the steps.

I've gone for a classic layered planting made up of trees, shrubs, perennials, and bulbs. To the right of the steps, I created a deep bed that measures 16–20ft (5–6m) deep, and into that, I've put a little terrace that gets the west sun. Here, beneath a Tibetan cherry tree, we've set out a tiny table and some chairs, as it's a great spot for an evening drink; the dappled light that filters through the tree onto the paving and table is absolutely stunning. Understanding where you get the best light and how that moves around the space really helps you squeeze more atmosphere out of your garden and make it extra special.

To the left of the steps, I have built a little office studio along the boundary wall; it gets really good morning light, which makes it a nice place to be early in the day. There's also a little terrace in front of it, with a small outdoor kitchen enclosed by plants. The office building is relatively small, so it doesn't cast a huge shadow over the garden or lose much light as the day goes on. I've fitted it with a little green sedum roof that the birds seem to love.

The view of the sitting area on the main terrace through the plants, which is shaded by an arching Tibetan cherry tree.

MIXED-SPECIES LAWN

In the central space, I felt a lawn would be wasted space. Although we don't have to worry about kids kicking around soccer balls, we do have lady dogs that leave marks on the grass. So, I managed to convince Mrs. Frost that I could put in a little species meadow here, too.

The lawn is about 13 x 40ft (4 x 12m) and has got a lot more grass species in it compared to the mini meadow, so it makes for a different habitat, is easier to maintain, and grows slower than a wildflower meadow. I've framed the mixed-species lawn with a mower's width of smart turf.

I've been reliably informed that if you measure all the gardens in the UK, apparently they add up to an area slightly smaller than New Jersey, so even if we do something small to help wildlife, collectively we can do a lot. Even Mrs. Frost, who prefers things tidy, has to admit that it does look nice.

I go over the main lawn with the mower at full height at the beginning of the growing season, then let it be when its rate of growth slows in midsummer. What's good is that while the lawn is unkempt in the middle, it has a neat border—the mowed edge defines it and simultaneously frames the ornamental planting in the borders that surround it. It was a bit of an experiment, but it works nicely. Even with just the couple of wilder areas that I've got, the diversity of plants is mind-blowing.

Just as in the front garden, I will add some bulbs and local flora to the lawn. Cowslips and oxslips provide pops of soft yellow and cream early in spring. Then, bulbs such as iris and crocus appear, which contrast beautifully in both color and shape when they overlap in flower. The crocus bulbs will naturalize and seed around. As the crocus and iris die down, *Narcissus canaliculatus* springs up to take their places. That's what I've done so far, but I'm constantly tinkering with the plants within the lawn and trying out new plants, combinations, and timings.

Grasses mix

Betony	Lady's bedstraw
Bird's foot trefoil	Lawn chamomile
Browntop bentgrass	Meadow buttercup
Bulbous buttercup	Meadow foxtail
Catsear	Oxeye daisy
Chewings fescue	Perennial ryegrass
Common daisy	Slender creeping red fescue
Common knapweed	Small-leaved Timothy
Common trefoil	Wild red clover
Crested dogstail	Yarrow
Hard fescue	Yellow oatgrass
Kidney vetch	Yellow rattle

This meadow mix is rich in grasses, so it's quite stable compared to a wildflower meadow and doesn't change from year to year.

*I'm constantly
tinkering with the
plants within
the lawn and trying
out new plants,
combinations,
and timings.*

Crocus tommasinianus

Early crocus

Height ¾–1½in (2–4cm) **Spread** 4in (10cm)
Time of flower Spring **Soil** Well-drained
Position Full sun/full shade/partial shade
Hardiness Hardy

I have been growing this crocus in the lawn
for years, and funnily enough, there is a
huge carpet of them across from my house
in front of our local church. It will seed
about and produce offsets, which it can
do fairly quickly, and that's what makes it
a favorite for naturalizing. It amazes me
that something so small and delicate is so
tough! If you are worried about spread,
it also works well in pots. As it tolerates
quite a lot of shade, I use it drifting out of
a woodland area, where it looks amazing.
They are early to flower and so are great
providers of nectar and pollen, which is
welcomed by insects after winter
hibernation. The slim, grass-like leaves
and tubular-shaped flowers vary in size,
just like their color—from soft lilac to
deeper purples. Other common names
include woodland crocus, and I have also
heard it called "Tommies," which makes
C. tommasinianus 'Whitewell Purple' or
'Lilac Beauty', and also *C. speciosus* 'Albus'.

Iris 'J.S. Dijt'

Iris 'J.S. Dijt'

Height 4–6in (10–15cm) **Spread** 4in (10cm)
Time of flower Spring **Soil** Moist but
well-drained **Position** Full sun/partial
shade **Hardiness** Hardy

This is another plant that I was introduced
to while working at Barnsdale Gardens for
Geoff Hamilton. It was used a lot in alpine
and screened areas to great effect. Planted
as a group, this iris brings a great variety
of color in spring. *Iris reticulata* is a bulb
native to Turkey, Iran, and parts of Russia,
where it grows in cooler mountain ranges,
open and alpine meadows, so that starts to
guide us as to what it loves. *Iris* 'J.S. Dijt' is a
lovely addition to the *reticulata* range; this
variety has mid-green foliage that reaches
4–6in (10–15cm) and flowers that are 3in
(8cm) across. It flowers in early spring, with
blooms that carry a soft fragrance and are
an intense plum-purple color with a
stunning white, yellow, blue, and deeper
purple throat. When I write that down, the
colors sound like they should not work, but
I promise you that they do! The flowers are
delightful, and when planted with *Crocus
tommasinianus*, they're stunning.

Narcissus 'Canaliculatus'
Daffodil 'Canaliculatus'

Height 6in (15cm) **Spread** 4in (10cm)
Time of flower Spring **Soil** Moist but
well-drained **Position** Full sun/partial
shade **Hardiness** Hardy

This is a *Narcissus tazetta* cultivar that
dates back to early 1900 and is one of the
oldest bulbs still for sale, which I think
says a lot about this dainty little thing. That
said, for a small plant, it still packs a punch,
with its blue-green foliage that holds well
vertically and doesn't flop in early spring.
It produces clusters of four or five stunning
flowers per stem that are made up of what
look like mini egg cups. These are a real
golden yellow, surrounded by pure white
outer petals that recede slightly from the
central cup and seem to accentuate it. For
a small bulb, they produce an amazingly
sweet fragrance. It only reaches roughly
6in (15cm) and likes a well-drained spot in
good light, so this petite plant works really
well in a pot, at the front of a border, or
I like to naturalize it in grass, which it's
more than happy to do. If you do this, let
it die back naturally and don't cut the lawn
too soon.

Primula veris
Common cowslip

Height 10in (25cm) **Spread** 4in (10cm)
Time of flower Spring **Soil** Moist but
well-drained **Position** Full sun/partial
shade **Hardiness** Hardy

I love that time of year when our
hedgerows come alive, and I wanted a little
of that at home—hence, primulas! I have
planted a couple of different species in
the lawn; first is the cowslip, *Primula veris*,
which is commonly seen where I live, but
they are declining (please don't ever dig
any up on your walks). It has so many
connections with English folklore and
tradition and is found in meadows,
woodland floors, and often hedgerows.
The stalks hold up dark green, wrinkled
leaves that will reach about 8in (20cm)
and yellow, nodding, bell-shaped flowers
that carry a lovely fragrance. When these
blooms appear, it is a sign to me that better
weather is on the way. The common
cowslip is a semi-evergreen perennial
that will grow in various soils, but it does
seem to love our local limestone.

Primula elatior
Oxlip

Height 6–8in (15–20cm) **Spread** 4in (10cm)
Time of flower Spring **Soil** Moist but
well-drained **Position** Full sun/partial
shade **Hardiness** Hardy

The second primula is the oxslip, *Primula
elatior*, which is a bit more of a challenge,
as it is a little fussy about its requirements,
but I grow it as an experiment in my
garden. It's found in abundance in England
in Suffolk, Essex, and Cambridgeshire, but
a lot of these areas do hold more moisture
in the ground than my garden and are in
partial shade. So, the first thing I did was
determine the damper and shadier areas
of my garden as prime spots to plant this.
That said, I have seen them flourishing in
more meadow-like settings, so what I call
my unkept lawn has become their new
home. This primula has an elegance about
it. It's a semi-evergreen perennial that
forms a basal rosette of leaves that are
green in color and oval in shape. In
mid-spring, softly hairy stems arise from
the base, carrying clusters of bell-shaped,
soft, pale yellow flowers. Just exquisite!

TREES AND SHRUBS

Between the lower and upper terraces, there is a change in height of 8ft (2.5m). So, to divide the space, I've introduced deep borders of trees and shrubs in front and behind the main terrace.

To help lead the eye, I've planted a selection of trees, including a giant dogwood (*Cornus controversa*), a *Malus* 'Evereste' crab apple, and an amelanchier on the house side. I've also placed a *Salix magnifica* willow and Tibetan cherry (*Prunus serrula*) on the other side of the main terrace, to help lead the eye from the lowest to the highest points in the garden and connect the two terraces. The trees on the mid terrace serve more than one purpose; they break the view from the lower to mid terraces, they provide structure through the garden, and they also help tie the terraces together and draw the eye from space to space.

I inherited a couple of trees that were already in the garden when we took it on, including the beautiful Tibetan cherry at the back of the main terrace, as well as a dark-leaved Japanese maple, *Acer plamatum* 'Bloodgood', in front of the garage. The acer is in totally and utterly the wrong position, so later in the summer, it gets absolutely scorched, but it's been there for around 20 years, and I don't have the heart to take it out. Funnily enough, it's ended up driving the whole color theme, and I've added some other plants in rich dark colors that help knit everything together. For example, I've planted a lovely elder called *Sambucus nigra* f. *porphyrophylla* 'Thundercloud' and the willow *Salix magnifica*, which has a beautiful dark stem and actually looks more like a magnolia. In one corner on the lower side of the main terrace, there is a Cornelian cherry (*Cornus mas*), which is a real bonus, especially when its stems turn a copper color as it gets older. The dark stem of the Tibetan cherry (*Prunus serrula*) has also become part of the scheme.

In terms of large shrubs and small trees, although I've got a quite a few, I've pruned them to lift their canopies so the planting doesn't feel too heavy. I'm aware that some people would balk at the idea of so many trees in a relatively small space, but they help link the various levels and make connections with trees outside the garden. They also create and frame views as you're walking along the main terrace.

I've also planted quite a few smaller shrubs, such as wilder-looking species roses in deep, rich colors through to whites and pinks, including *Rosa* 'Dunwich Rose' (SpH) and *Rosa* 'Cardinal de Richelieu'. I've also included a *Magnolia* x *loebneri* 'Merrill', although I'm really growing that as a multi-stem tree.

The darker leaves of 'Thundercloud' contrast with the green foliage, drawing the eye comfortably to the red peonies.

Amelanchier lamarckii
Snowy mespilus

Height 13ft (4m) **Spread** 10ft (3m) **Time of flower** Spring
Soil Moist but well-drained **Position** Full sun/partial shade
Hardiness Fully hardy

This is a very versatile small tree, and it is a bit of a must
for any garden, as it is one of the most useful—not just
because of the ease of care it offers but because it carries
you through the seasons. Mid-spring sees clusters of
delicate white flowers that provide a charming show and
are set against soft, bronze-tinged emerging foliage that
matures into soft green, oval leaves. After flowering, dark
round fruit adds another layer of interest and food for the
birds, a sight that is lovely to watch through my kitchen
window. The foliage then turns a rich mix of orange and
deep red in fall. I normally buy this as a multi-stem, which
really does seem to suit the natural form of the tree. If
you are using this in smaller spaces, it clips really well into
a soft umbrella shape. It will work in most types of soil,
but although the advice is to avoid really limey soils, mine
is a little limey, and my trees are really happy. However, it
does get a good mulch and was planted into a nutritious,
well-drained garden soil.

Amelanchier lamarckii

Cornus controversa

Malus 'Evereste'

Cornus controversa
Giant dogwood

Height 10–23ft (3–7m) **Spread** 26ft (8m) **Time of flower** Spring **Soil** Most types **Position** Full sun/partial shade **Hardiness** Fully hardy

Cornus, for me, has become a bit of a go-to over the years. It tends to be a hard-working plant and is quite low maintenance in terms of needs. The two I have in the garden are my favorites, one being the *Cornus mas* and the other being this one. Its alternative common name is the wedding cake tree because as it matures, the layers create a wonderful tiered effect. Mine is planted not far from the house, so it can be viewed from a couple of windows, which makes this tree part of daily life. It's a small tree that really adds structure to a border or can work well as a single focal point. You will see a mix of colors within its branches as the years go on; the leaves are a dark green with a sheen, and the underside sports a blue tinge, which come fall turns a deep ruby red. In later spring, good-sized, umbellifer white flowers sit along the horizontal stems, and as these die, dark berries start to develop, which last well into fall. I have found the tree will tolerate most soils.

Malus 'Evereste'
Crab apple 'Evereste'

Height 13–20ft (4–6m) **Spread** 13–26ft (4–8m) **Time of flower** Spring **Soil** Moist but well-drained **Position** Full sun **Hardiness** Fully hardy

So many of the ornamental apples are stunning, but if I could only have one—which, to be fair, is all I have room for—it would be this one! It is just a really good all-round tree. Its springtime display is a joy; buds start a pinky-red and then open to a pure white flower that lasts for a good amount of time. The foliage is green with a silk finish, which come fall provides a beautiful golden display. After the flowers come small crab apples, which color-wise remind me of 'Cox's Orange Pippin'—another of my favorites. The fruits will last all winter and provide food for visiting birds. This is another tree that I like growing as a multi-stem, as it reacts well to clipping and shaping. 'Evereste' will tolerate most soils and is great for a smaller space, but it generally works in so many settings!

95

Prunus serrula
Tibetan cherry

Height 26–39ft (8–12m) **Spread** 26ft (8m)
Time of flower Summer **Soil** Moist but
well-drained **Position** Full sun **Hardiness**
Fully hardy

Introduced in 1908 and very popular,
although quite unusual, this cherry is
grown mainly for its bark rather than its
flower. It's not a heavy tree, so it provides
lovely dappled shade—I have planted
it by a seating area where the shadow
patterns are stunning when the sun comes
through the canopy. The bark peels and is
mahogany in color and is also incredibly
tactile. I tend to grow this as a multi-stem
just to get more from the bark. For me,
it's a tree that works through all of the
seasons. The leaves are green, slim, and
a little willow-like, and in late spring, a rich
yellow-white flower adds a moment to
the seasonal interest. Growing in full sun
will help this display, but if you're looking
for the famous cherry blossom, this one is
not for you! It's happy in most soils—just
make sure the drainage is reasonable. If
you really want the best from the tree, an
annual washing of the bark will help.

Rosa 'Cardinal de Richelieu'
Rose 'Cardinal de Richelieu'

Height 5ft (1.5m) **Spread** 4ft (1.2m)
Time of flower Summer **Soil** Most types
Position Full sun/partial shade **Hardiness**
Fully hardy

I think this was one of the first roses that
really wowed me, so much so that I used
it in my first RHS Chelsea Flower Show
garden. I'm very drawn to its rich colors. It's
a 'gallica' shrub rose, first introduced in the
1840s, and as a group these date back to
the Romans and Greeks. Members of this
group tend to be shorter shrub plants, and
this variety has a relaxed habit and next to
no thorns. The clusters of flowers carry
you through June and July and are velvety
and dark purple in color, and as they fully
open, they become ball-like in form. The
fragrance is quite light, and the flowers sit
well against the dark green foliage. It is a
versatile plant; its habit means it is really
easy to interplant, and it's happy in sun or
partial shade and grows in most soils. On
top of that, the blooms cut well for a
bouquet inside!

Rosa 'Celestial'
Rose 'Celestial'

Height 6ft (1.8m) **Spread** 4ft (1.2m)
Time of flower Summer **Soil** Most types
Position Full sun/partial shade **Hardiness**
Fully hardy

This beauty dates back to the 1810s, and
I think it has seen the test of time. It's a
classy classic, a little black dress—well, not
that little, as it will get to roughly 6ft (1.8m).
That said, it's a tough plant, so you can
control its growth. Happy in sun or partial
shade, it seems to tolerate most soils and
works well as a stand-alone specimen or
within an old hedge. The foliage is a soft
gray-green and works so well with the
flower, which is a delight from bud to fully
opening. It's a semi-double, mellow-pink
rose with eye-catching yellow stamens.
The fragrance is rich—a real old rose! The
whole thing has a relaxed feel to it. I have
found it to be a really heathy rose; I think
it's up there with the best of the old roses,
and my garden would not be the same
without it.

Rosa forrestiana
Forrest's rose

Height 6ft (1.8m) **Spread** 6ft (1.8m) **Time of
flower** Summer **Soil** Most types **Position**
Full sun **Hardiness** Fully hardy

A lovely old rose, introduced in 1899.
For a wild rose, this one has a bright
flower that is deep fuchsia in color,
with creamy yellow stamens. It has a
small window of flowering in summer, but
the attractive blooms are held in dense
clusters. Its foliage is fine and green with
a purple hint, set on a shrub that holds a
flask-like shape. The flowers are followed
by decorative hips, which add interest to
the plant through fall and winter.

Rosa 'Hebe's Lip'

Rose 'Hebe's Lip'

Height 6–6½ft (1.8–2m) **Spread** 5ft (1.5m) **Time of flower** Summer–fall **Soil** Most types **Position** Full sun/partial shade **Hardiness** Fully hardy

Some would say this modest rose can be a little susceptible to disease (although I think good garden practices and thoughtful positioning help avoid this), but even so, it's one of my favorite old Damask roses, and one of the oldest, introduced pre-1700. It's not in your face; its semi-double blooms are attractive and elegant—a creamy white with tips touched with crimson, as if a little "lipstick" has been applied before a night out. It's a rose that just makes me smile, and although it only flowers once, the blooms arrive in clusters en masse, and the fragrance is a rich musk that will stop you in your tracks. It carries strong red hips that last well into winter. It is a compact, thorny shrub with mid to dark green foliage with serrated edges. It tolerates most soils and tolerates a little shade.

Rosa 'Hebe's Lip'

Rosa 'Kazanlik'

Rosa 'Kazanlik'
Rose 'Kazanlik'

Height 6–6½ft (1.8–2m) **Spread** 5ft (1.5m)
Time of flower Summer–fall **Soil** Most
types **Position** Full sun/partial shade
Hardiness Fully hardy

When I look at this flower, I just want to
jump in! It has a soft, luxurious feel, and
I think it would make a great mattress,
but it's not just how it looks—it is also
very fragrant. The blooms are double but
relaxed, a soft, light pink with nearly white
undertones in color, and arrive in clusters.
The stems are well-armed with prickles,
but I like that, and the foliage is light green.
Although the plant will reach about 6 to
6½ft (1.8 to 2m), it can be manipulated to
suit your space. It is a good, vigorous rose,
introduced pre-1700, which will tolerate
poorer soils and handle some shade. Just
remember, it flowers on old wood, so only
prune it after flowering if you need to.

Rosa 'Joan Beales'

Rosa 'Joan Beales'
Rose 'Joan Beales'

Height 3ft (90cm) **Spread** 3ft (90cm) **Time of flower**
Summer–fall **Soil** Most types **Position** Full sun/partial shade
Hardiness Fully hardy

This is a modern shrub (introduced in 2004) that is unique to
the UK. It bears elegant semi-double blooms that are a deep
velvety red color and have a fantastic fragrance. The foliage is
dark, and when young ,it has a beet-colored tint. Tolerant of
shade and suitable to be planted in a container, it's a beautiful
rose in many positions in the garden. For best results, mulch
in late winter and, to improve flowering, apply a balanced
fertilizer in late winter or early spring, then repeat in early
summer. This rose is bred by Peter Beales, the much-
respected expert and breeder of roses, and is named for his
late wife and co-founder of Peter Beales Roses.

Rosa 'Nuits de Young'
Rose 'Nuits de Young'

Height 4ft (1.2m) **Spread** 3ft (90cm) **Time of flower** Summer–fall **Soil** Most types **Position** Full sun/partial shade **Hardiness** Fully hardy

Moss roses definitely seemed to be a favorite of the Victorians, as was this one, which was introduced in 1845, and I love the pure quality of their petals. The stems on these plants are also something special, and as the bud develops, it carries a kind of red/brown moss all the way down the stem that helps make the moss roses easier to identify. 'Nuits de Young' is a compact plant, and I have used it as a low hedge in the past, where it works well. The blooms carry a good old-rose fragrance (if that makes sense!) and are a rich, dark-maroon color that you can more or less feel. I have always thought it would make a wonderful shade of paint. At the center of all that glory are near-gold stamens that sit within a tidy, dark foliage. Carried on strong, upright growth, it's a rose that will tolerate a poorer soil, and while it likes full sun, I think a little shade helps the flower last longer.

Rosa 'Dunwich Rose' (SpH)
Rose 'Dunwich Rose'

Height 24in (60cm) **Spread** 3ft (90cm) **Time of flower** Spring–summer **Soil** Most types **Position** Full sun/partial shade **Hardiness** Fully hardy

This is an elegant, early flowering rose that has been around since 1950. It's not just the flowers that I love but its habit, too; 'Dunwich Rose' has arching stems, and its colored stamens and fern-like foliage create a lovely dome. The flower is delicate, single, and a pure white with a lemon center, and when in bloom, they cover the whole of the plant en masse. The flowers are followed by small, almost-black hips in the fall. This rose can handle a good amount of shade, and it will tolerate poorer soils. Because of its compact nature, it makes a great low, even hedge.

Salix gracilistyla 'Mount Aso'
Willow 'Mount Aso'

Height 8–13ft (2.5–4m) **Spread** 8–13ft (2.5–4m) **Time of flower** Late winter–early spring **Soil** Moist but well-drained **Position** Full sun **Hardiness** Fully hardy

So many *Salix* are known for their winter stems, but for me, this one just has something a little more. That extra interest comes by way of "beehive"-shaped, soft, fluffy, red-pink catkins that cloak the stems in late winter and early spring. These little things are so tactile and play beautifully with winter light. That said, I also think it looks great in full leaf—the leaves are narrow and have a blue-green sheen that stays surprisingly fresh throughout summer, with the underside carrying a silvery finish. Added to that, this plant has a multi-stemmed structure, meaning it provides a super foil for other planting—it's also a plant that Mrs. Frost cuts the winter stems from for the house. It will reach over 13ft (4m) if left to its own devices, but I cut back my plants every 2 or 3 years once they have established stems to keep them in check. It's happy in full sun or partial shade in my garden, but it will tolerate a wetter spot if necessary. I have seen this planted en masse in a larger space, and it looks amazing. Overall, it's a hard-working, low-maintenance shrub.

Salix magnifica
Foot-catkin willow

Height 10ft (3m) **Spread** 8–10ft (2.5–3m) **Time of flower** Spring **Soil** Most types **Position** Full sun/partial shade **Hardiness** Fully hardy

At a quick glance, you might think this willow is a magnolia because the leaves are that big and shaped. It's a good upright plant that has an open habit, so it does make a nice small tree over time. The foliage works well against stems that carry tones of red and purple. The plant will hold your attention, with reddish-brown shoots that open into the large leaves that have gorgeous veining. As the plant matures, so do the catkins, reaching up to 8in (20cm) long, that follow soon after the leaves. As the catkins open, they start as a red color and then fade to yellow. *Salix magnifica* really does carry its name well, and if you grow it, give a little thought to where you plant it and put some love into the soil.

Rosa 'Nuits de Young'

Salix gracilistyla 'Mount Aso'

Rosa 'Dunwich Rose' (SpH)

Salix magnifica

HERBACEOUS PLANTING

When I worked for the Parks Department the planting was in the style of Victorian parks—rose beds, hydrangeas, and annuals. We were slowly changing this and using more herbaceous plants, but it was working for Geoff Hamilton that really opened up that world for me.

Like most people, when I started gardening, I was interested mainly in flowers. However, over time, things have changed, including both the way that gardens are viewed and the way they are maintained. Nowadays, for me, it's less about the beauty of the flowers—I view this really as a bonus—and more about what a plant will bring to the party in terms of form and texture.

Take peonies; I think they're a great reminder that gardens are about taking time to enjoy special moments. Lots of people I talk to about peonies say that while they are really lovely, they're gone all too quickly. I always respond that they're missing the point; the thing is to celebrate these plants for the period of time in which they are absolute perfection. It's the same with asparagus; the flavor of the spears in season is just incredible and incomparable to those that have been shipped halfway around the world in the middle of December. It's always good to remember to just pause and really savor that moment.

These days, I try to have the same approach with herbaceous plants. I relish the moments when they are at their most special. Herbaceous planting can create a wonderful sort of undulated mid to lower layer in the garden. It's a bit like a big quilt that softens everything and makes connections between the ground level and upper layers. These plants bring life, too, as many of them attract wildlife by providing so much for them.

My main structural herbaceous planting is a mix of two things: the plants that know their job and new plants that I constantly seem to be on the hunt for. For the herbaceous perennial layer in the main terrace, I've chosen some very hard-working plants that have reliably performed for me over the years, such as *Phlomis russeliana, Euphorbia schillingii*, and *Geranium* 'Blue Cloud'. I've also added

The vertical spires of *Delphinium requienii* sing against the lush green backdrop.

Digitalis, euphorbia, astrantias, and baltic parsley. Lovely combination.

biennials, which have a lifespan of a couple of years, along with some short-lived perennials that tend to seed themselves around naturally. I don't want these choices to be showy, so they are mostly driven by species or native plants. I love the freedom that these plants bring to the garden, the way they change the picture year after year.

The structural herbaceous planting is a mix of two things: good workers that turn up and do a job balanced with new plants that I constantly seem to be on the hunt for. I do include ornamental grasses into this mix, too, such as *Molinia* 'Skyracer'. Grasses prove that not everything in your garden needs to be a star. They bring movement and interact with light magically, creating a canvas that brings other plants center stage.

I've now started to introduce bulbs into this part of the garden, including the species tulips *Tulipa turkestanica* and *Tulipa sylvestris*. There are some native daffodils dotted around, too, as well as quite a lot of drumstick alliums (*Allium sphaerocephalon*), and I plan to put in a load of camassias, particularly *Camassia leichtlinii* 'Blue Candle'. All together, the whole feeling is quite romantic and like a good love song.

Angelica taiwaniana

Height 4–6ft (1.2–1.8m) **Spread** 3ft (1m) **Time of flower**
Summer **Soil** Most types **Position** Sun/partial shade
Hardiness Hardy

This plant is a member of a group of umbellifers that has
become a bit of a favorite of mine over the years. You will
now find a huge array of *Angelica* species available; some
are biennial, some are short-lived perennials, but all are
striking. The stems and bracts of this variety, *Angelica
taiwaniana,* have a purple tinge and carry scented, creamy
white flowers that form small globes. The seeds produced
are also fragrant and will set easily. It is amazing how you
can change the feeling of your garden on a yearly basis
with these self-seeding plants; I enjoy seeing where nature
takes the plants, but that may not be everybody's style.
They can be a short-lived perennial—although some
varieties live longer than others—but once you have this
plant in the garden, it is easy to keep it going, especially in
sun or semi-shade, where it is most happy.

Angelica taiwaniana

Bistorta amplexicaulis 'Firetail'

Bistorta amplexicaulis 'Firetail'
Red bistort

Height 4ft (1.2m) **Spread** 3ft (90cm) **Time of flower** Summer–fall **Soil** Moist but well-drained **Position** Full sun/partial shade **Hardiness** Fully hardy

Advances in science mean that botanists can now analyze plant DNA and recategorize plants into their correct families, which, in turn, means that some plants are being renamed. This plant is one such; once known as *Persicaria*, it is now called *Bistorta*. These plants have become pretty popular, as there is a good diversity of colors and sizes among the species. With 'Firetail', it's the tone of the flower that pulls me back to it, as the crimson color is really vivid. The blooms themselves are made up of tiny clusters that create a long, thin spike sitting on strong stems that arrive in midsummer, hang around well into fall, and are a magnet for pollinating insects. The plant is clump-forming and carries handsome, heart-shaped, mid-green leaves with strong veins. *Bistorta amplexicaulis* adds structure to your borders and is happy in sun or partial shade. It's an easy plant to work with and contributes a good amount of visual interest for a large part of the year. You may read that it prefers damper soils, but I have added good amounts of organic matter, and it works well in my drier garden—I just don't tend to use it in the really hot parts.

Digitalis parviflora

Digitalis parviflora
Foxglove

Height 2–2½ft (60–80cm) **Spread** 12in (30cm) **Time of flower** Summer **Soil** Most types **Position** Full sun/dappled shade/partial shade **Hardiness** Fully hardy

I think it was Nick Hamilton at Barnsdale Gardens who first got me into *Digitalis*, and then over years of building gardens at the RHS Chelsea Flower Show, they have become a bit of a go-to, as many work well at that time of year. But this one is a little different from the foxgloves we know and love—you could even say it looks a little dark and exotic—and it's well worth a place in the garden. It has dark-green, narrow leaves that have a glossy finish and are carried all the way up the strong stem, from which they curve elegantly. Stems are topped with brownish-orange flowers that have a lovely dark tip to them and that are densely packed to create a lovely spike. It looks wonderful with *Deschampsia*. It is happy in partial shade, but it will take some sun if it's in good garden soil. I mulch my plants, as they like it neither too dry nor too wet. It's quite easy to grow from seed and will come true from seed, too.

Euphorbia cyparissias 'Fens Ruby'
Cypress spurge

Height 12in (30cm) **Spread** Indefinite **Time of flower** Spring–summer **Soil** Light, well-drained **Position** Full sun **Hardiness** Fully hardy

This is one of those plants that is not everyone's style, but in the right place, it is a great little worker. The foliage is a mass of thin, needle-like leaves that seem to vary in color, depending on the light. I have seen it as anything from a dark bluish-gray to a rich maroon flush. It can make a really effective groundcover, traveling across the soil with short running stems. In late spring to early summer, the flowers arrive with lime-green bracts that pop against the dark foliage. It's happy in sun or partial shade in well-drained soil, but do plant this where you are happy for it to spread, as it can be a bit of a nuisance in the wrong spot. I tend to plant it where I can contain its travel. In fall, this little pile of bottlebrushes turns the most amazing yellow. Be careful, though, as this can be a skin and eye irritant.

Euphorbia schillingii
Schilling spurge

Height 3ft (1m) **Spread** 24in (60cm) **Time of flower** Summer–early fall **Soil** Moist but free-draining **Position** Full sun/partial shade **Hardiness** Fully hardy

I have been growing this for some years, and it is a favorite in my designs, as it really draws the eye, plus it's great as foil for other plants. This euphorbia works hard all season, from lush early stems that look near sub-tropical, to the spear-shaped, rich green leaves that seem to change with the seasons and carry a central rib, which is a lovely little detail. The stems turn a red-brown in winter and hold good structure. The bracts are a vivid lime green in late spring to early summer, providing a bold contrast to the foliage, with a flat, open feel, lasting until the back end of summer. It's not very demanding—it is happy in sun or partial shade—but if I do plant it in the sun, I make sure that I mulch the soil well. I cut it back in February and then mulch, but if the clump gets a bit heavy, I lift it, then divide and replant.

Francoa sonchifolia 'Molly Anderson'
Wedding flower

Height 2–3ft (60–90cm) **Spread** 12in (30cm) **Time of flower** Summer **Soil** Well-drained **Position** Full sun/partial shade **Hardiness** Frost hardy

This, for me, is a wonderful genus of herbaceous perennials that seems to be a little underused. It's from a group that I first came across while working for Geoff Hamilton, and it took me a while to get my head around how to use it. *Francoa sonchifolia* 'Molly Anderson' has deeply lobed green leaves that give a really strong form and spikes of pink flowers with dark-pink to reddish markings that sit high above the foliage, a little like bottlebrushes in looks. I like positioning it at the front of the border, but not in isolation, where, if repeated, it will really draw the eye. It will grow happily in sun or partial shade, and the flowers are really attractive to bees, which gives them great value in the garden.

Galatella linosyris
Goldilocks

Height 20in (50cm) **Spread** 16in (40cm) **Time of flower** Late summer–fall **Soil** Most types, well-drained **Position** Full sun/partial shade **Hardiness** Fully hardy

When I first saw this, it was labeled *Aster linosyris* and was in the booth of Hardy's Cottage Garden Plants at a show; Rosy Hardy explained that it was an unusual British native. Needless to say, it came home with me, as I thought it was utterly charming, and I have had fun with it ever since. It grows happily in the gravel garden, where it looks very naturalistic, but it also looks at home in the mixed border. I have it interplanted with *Campanula* and *Delphinium requienii*, which both sit below *Euphorbia mellifera*. In the wild, it is found on the west side of the country and on limestone cliffs, rocky slopes, and open, grassy habitats. It is a hardy little thing, happy in sun and in reasonably well-drained soil. Its slender stems are clothed in fine gray-green foliage early in the year, and the plant has a real tactile pull. In the summer, it bears clusters of slightly unkempt but rather beautiful golden-yellow flowers that look like mini pincushions, which pollinators seem to love.

Euphorbia cyparissias 'Fens Ruby'

Francoa sonchifolia 'Molly Anderson'

Euphorbia schillingii

Galatella linosyris

Geranium 'Blue Cloud'

Cranesbill 'Blue Cloud'

Height 28in (70cm) **Spread** 3ft (1m) **Time of flower** Spring–summer **Soil** Moist but well-drained **Position** Full sun/partial shade **Hardiness** Fully hardy

Reading this book, you have probaby figured out that I do like a geranium! That's because they are hard-working plants, and with the number available, you can find one to work in most conditions. 'Blue Cloud' is a welcome addition; it has not been around that long, but it has quickly become a bit of a star. It produces soft, loose mounds of finely divided green leaves and pale blue flowers with delightful darker veining, flowering its heart out for months. I first fell in love with planting this with *Paeonia* 'Bowl of Beauty', having been given a plant and literally popping it into a gap in the border. The two together look great, and I have been doing it ever since! This geranium also works really well with roses. Once it has finished flowering, I cut the whole plant to nearly ground level, and it soon returns with a lovely new flush of growth. I also dig it up and divide it in fall or spring every few years to keep it healthy.

Geranium × oxonianum 'Katherine Adele'

Cranesbill 'Katherine Adele'

Height 16in (40cm) **Spread** 16in (40cm) **Time of flower** Summer **Soil** Most types **Position** Full sun/partial shade **Hardiness** Fully hardy

This plant is doing a lovely job of growing between steps in my garden, and it looks super at the front of the border. For me, it only gets to 12–16in (30–40cm) high, and as lovely as the flower is, which is a pinky white with dark veins, it is the foliage that I use the plant for, which really catches the eye. The center of the leaves starts as a deep burgundy wine color with a soft green outer edge, which fades as the year goes on. You can cut the plant back after flowering, and it soon refreshes itself. It has a comfortable feel and naturalizes really well, so it is easy to plant with. Happy in sun or partial shade and most garden soils, this geranium is definitely one for the wildlife.

Molinia caerulea subsp. arundinacea 'Skyracer'

Purple moor grass 'Skyracer'

Height 2–3ft (60–90cm) **Spread** 12in (30cm) **Time of flower** Summer **Soil** Well-drained **Position** Full sun/partial shade **Hardiness** Fully hardy

I think *Molinia* is one of the best grasses to work with, and this one is a British native tall moor grass. Although *Molinia* grows on riverbanks and marshlands and prefers cooler, moist conditions, I have found that this plant deals with most soil conditions. I love the way the flower stems sit well above the foliage, which is mid-green and neat and tidy. With the arrival of the stems comes its architectural presence. Stems can reach up to 6½ft (2m), and the stalks and flowers are green with slender flowers, but, come fall, both turn a warm tan color that looks wonderful in sunlight throughout the year, so it is really worth thinking about where you plant this— whether in the morning sun or to catch the sun as it goes down.

Paeonia 'Buckeye Belle'

Peony 'Buckeye Belle'

Height 3ft (90cm) **Spread** 20in (50cm) **Time of flower**
Summer **Soil** Moist but well-drained **Position** Full sun/
partial shade **Hardiness** Fully hardy

I think the herbaceous perennial peony is a wonderful
reminder that gardens are about fleeting but beautiful
moments. The form of the plant is great to work with, the
leaves carry a strong shape, and I have never had to stake
the tall stems. 'Buckeye Belle' has dark-green foliage with
a sheen finish, and as we move into fall, the leaves turn a
glorious deep ruby-red that lasts for a good while. It's one
that will take a little shade, and if I'm honest, I think the
flowers benefit from not being in the midday sun. The
blooms arrive in late May/early June and are a wonderful
deep red with golden stamens. The contrast with the
foliage is stunning, and they also make lovely bouquets
for the house. The plant does like a fertile soil with
half-decent drainage. In the garden, it is just sat under
the canopy of the dark foliage of *Sambucus nigra*
'Thundercloud', as they make a super pairing. If you want
a little drama in your garden, this one can easily grab your
attention. Another couple that I love are 'Bowl of Beauty',
which is a lovely soft pink with a white center, and
'Claire de Lune', which has pale lemon petals with rich
yellow stamens.

Phlomis russeliana
Turkish sage

Height 3ft (1m) **Spread** 3ft (90cm) **Time of flower** Spring–late summer **Soil** Moist but well-drained **Position** Full sun **Hardiness** Fully hardy

I think this plant is a dream to design with, as it works so well with other plants and you never feel it has to take center stage. Mind you, that's not to say that this variety lacks great qualities. First, I think it has real presence and does bring a little of the Mediterranean to the garden. The heart-shaped evergreen leaves are highly textured and offer a silvery touch. They cover the ground well, and their upright stems push up through the foliage, carrying eye-catching whorls of soft yellow-hooded flowers that last well into later summer. If you leave them after flowering, you will be provided with winter structure in the form of deep-brown, ornamental seedheads that ring the stems. You will enjoy watching the birds gather their seeds. Keep an eye out for a cold snap, as a good frost really adds to the scene. It works in so many settings; is happy in a warm, mixed border, interplanted with ornamental grasses; and is super in the gravel garden. It seems to be a long-lived plant that is happy in a sunny spot with decent drainage and is really good for year-round interest.

Valeriana montana
Mountain valerian

Height 8in (20cm) **Spread** 8in (20cm) **Time of flower** Spring–summer **Soil** Most types **Position** Full sun/partial shade **Hardiness** Fully hardy

I only came across *Valeriana montana* a few years ago, but it is a winner and shows the diversity of this species. This variety comes from the rocky slopes of Europe, which means it is tough and seems to do well in poorer soils. Its flower lasts better in a cooler spot, but the plant still likes reasonable light, so it is best positioned in an open space. It has a lovely habit—it sort of clumps and mounds while covering the ground well—and the olive-green leaves have a soft shine. Like other *Valeriana*, it's loved by pollinators. At home, I have used it between open stone steps, which mimics the look of the plant in its natural habitat. It flowers around April to May and produces elegant, dome-shaped heads that are a mellow pinky-white. The plant only reaches about 8in (20cm) in height, which makes it great for small spaces.

Valeriana pyrenaica
Capon's tail grass

Height 3–5ft (1–1.5m) **Spread** 24in (60cm) **Time of flower** Spring–summer **Soil** Moist but well-drained **Position** Full sun/partial shade **Hardiness** Fully hardy

Valeriana officinalis, which is known as common valerian, dates back to Greek and Roman times. It is a plant that I have used for years, as it piqued my interest and got me looking for different varieties. *V. officinalis* is an upright plant, with flower stems that reach up to 5ft (1.6m). It is not a heavy plant, as the foliage sits lower, and the pinnate-shaped leaves have a shine, carry a scent, and, because of its slender growth and low foliage, does not obstruct anything behind it. The flowers are borne in small clusters and come in whites and soft pinks. It was probably one of the first plants I started experimenting with as far as just letting plants loose in the garden, free to seed, then editing them to try to achieve a softer, wilder feel. *Valeriana pyrenaica,* which is native to the Pyrenees, is one of the first varieties I came across; it is a complex, very different beast than the standard *Valeriana*, starting with larger heart-shaped leaves that look as if they should be by the water's edge. The leaves clump up really well and provide an excellent background to plant against. It does seem happy in sun or partial shade, but I tend to work some organic matter into the soil just to get it into a moisture-retentive state. Purple-tinged stems rise above the foliage in early summer, with lacy umbels of soft, pollen-rich lilac flowers. As the flowers fade, soft, open clouds of seedheads appear that are quite magical. The plant does seed around, but not heavily, so although it's quite tall, I love to use it at the front of a border, as it really is eye-catching, popping up in gaps between other plants.

UPPER TERRACE WRAP

GRAVEL GARDEN:

"Wonderful Tonight," Eric Clapton

It's the end of the day, things are calming down, and I get to spend a little time with Mrs. Frost. The area has the feel of feet in warm sand, enjoying a early evening drink with someone you love, so the song here had to be "Wonderful Tonight."

UPPER TERRACE WRAP AND GREENHOUSE:

"Dreamy Skies," The Rolling Stones

This is a part of the garden that I can escape to— anyone who has a greenhouse will know what I mean! It's somewhere you can just lose time for a while and be by yourself. I think the Stones capture that sentiment in "Dreamy Skies."

The third level of the garden is the upper terrace, which is accessed by steps that lead from the main terrace, becoming lighter with a substantial retaining wall to the right. Once you reach the top of the steps, turn right and head up a few more steps, and you will arrive at a mini gravel garden surrounded by further layers of trees, shrubs, and varied herbaceous planting.

In front of the gravel garden, which marks the start of the upper terrace, is a big border that horticulturally links to the main terrace, which you can see looking up the garden. It not only screens the gravel garden but provides a backdrop to the mid-terrace planting. Here, I've planted an amelanchier, which picks up on the one on the lower terrace.

Behind is another small retaining wall, and along this runs a low hedge that I'm cloud pruning, which not only encloses and screens the top area really nicely but also prevents the planting on the border encroaching on the upper gravel space. Visually, the pruned shapes tie in with the clipped forms of the yew lower down in the garden. Interestingly, there's a point as you go up through the arches where you get a view along the hedge, and because you can see through the planting, which forms quite a strong line, it helps your eye along it.

The lower retaining wall has slightly raised the gravel garden so that it sits on a bit of a platform. It has a wall around one side and the back of it, then there is a step up, adding extra interest to the movement. Beyond the gravel garden is another low retaining wall, which contains a little woodland garden.

I know having a gravel garden and woodland next to each other might seem odd, but it really does work, perhaps because the gravel area is fully wrapped by plants, drifting in and out of the space. Or maybe it has to do with the simplicity of the colors. Woodlanders are among my very favorite plants, and I can never have enough of them; I sometimes think that if I could only grow one group of plants—say, if I were left on a desert island—it would have to be woodland plants!

In the far left corner of the garden sits my greenhouse, which is partly screened by a lifted hawthorn hedge. In front is a small gravel space that feels like a tiny courtyard, with just enough room for a small bistro table, which is great for picking out seeds, sowing, and sitting at with a cup of coffee!

A meandering path takes you through the gravel garden, where I like to relax and enjoy the evening sun with Mrs. Frost.

GRAVEL GARDEN

The most famous and inspiring gravel garden of all is probably that of the late, great gardener Beth Chatto, which she created at her home near Colchester, in Essex. Reading her early books and visiting this garden, as well as many other gardens devoted to drought-resistant plants, have really inspired me when designing similar gardens.

When I found myself living in one of the driest parts of the country, I couldn't help but want to experiment with this type of gardening. I think I made my first dry garden about 25 years ago, and I have been lucky enough to design these in hot dry climates across the world, including two in Egypt, one in the Atlas Mountains in Morocco, and one in the South of France. Even when I'm on vacation in sunny places, I can't help but look at wild plants and try to figure out what growing conditions they are thriving in.

Having a gravel garden means you can really widen the diversity of your planting and open up a new world of possibilities. Dry-climate plants are a fascinating group of plants to explore. As always, I tend to be predominantly interested in their shapes, forms, and finishes.

The area where I decided to put my gravel garden is open to the south and west, so it gets really baked in the summer, and because it's almost the highest part in the garden, it also has the most free-draining soil.

Visually, this gravel terrace sits in isolation from the rest of the garden. It is slightly hidden by the border in front of it, and I like the fact that when you're in the lower terraces, you can see there's something there because of the height of the plants, but you can't actually see what it is. It's not revealed until you go up the steps and through the arches, then it comes as quite a nice surprise. In some ways, it has a similar impact as the courtyard and the feeling of "Oh, I wasn't expecting that!"

Once you've reached this part of the garden, you're about 8ft (2.5m) up from the lower terrace, and your perspective on the garden as a whole totally changes. Standing up there, you get a lovely view of all the old cottage rooftops around our house, which are made from Collyweston stone and have beautiful stone chimneys in slightly different designs. It's not your average roofline, but it's an incredible piece of craftsmanship that I really enjoy looking at.

Planting Plan

Trees and Shrubs

- *Ilex crenata* (hedging)
- *Callistemon pityoides*
- *Calycanthus* 'Aphrodite'
- *Cornus mas*
- *Euonymus nanus* var. *turkestanicus*
- *Muehlenbeckia astonii*
- *Rosa* 'Dunwich Rose' (SpH)

Perennials

- *Alchemilla caucasica*
- *Achillea* 'Inca Gold'
- *Galatella linosyris*
- *Crithmum maritimum*
- *Eryngium* x *tripartitum*
- *Geranium* 'Ivan'
- *Kniphofia* 'Little Maid'
- *Limonium platyphyllum*
- *Molinia caerulea* subsp. *arundinacea* 'Skyracer'
- *Phlomis russeliana*
- *Pratia pedunculata*
- *Sedum aizoon* 'Euphorbioides'
- *Veronica gentianoides*

Drifts

Acis autumnalis 'September Snow'

Nicotiana sylvestris

Oenothera biennis

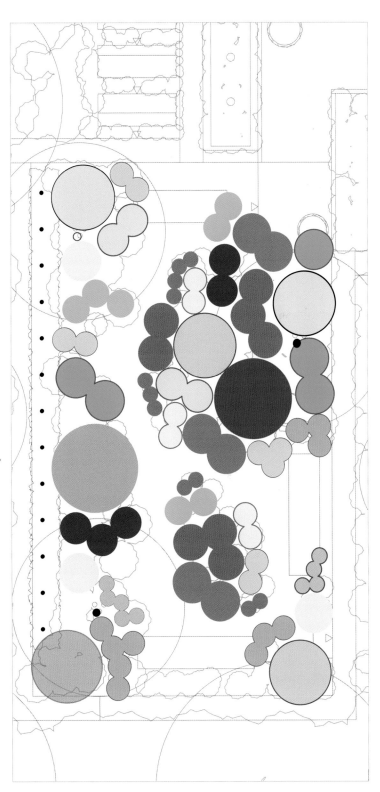

Prepping this area for planting was really easy. I added a load of topsoil, well-rotted manure, and gravel and just dug it all in, then once the plants had been put in, I dressed the surface around them with more gravel. Initially, I put the gravel down in a layer to a depth of around 1in (30mm), then as that naturally worked its way down into the soil over the first 12–18 months, I topped it off. I repeat this periodically every 2–3 years to keep a neat layer of gravel on the beds. I don't put any membrane down first, because you just end up with a lovely little seed bed beneath the gravel anyway, and as it's not a big area, it's easy to keep on top of any weeds that make their way up.

For the planting, I started out by peppering some trees and rather large shrubs through the space. For instance, I've got a couple of cornelian cherries (*Cornus mas*), which I've used for their rich brown bark more than anything else. As for shrubs, I've got wiggy-wig bush (*Muehlenbeckia astonii*), some *Calycanthus* 'Aphrodite', and a lovely *Euonymus nanus* var. *turkestanicus* up there. Then, I've been playing with all sorts of plants that can take a bit of dry semi-shade and others that are happy to be in the baking sun all day long.

As you go up the steps to the gravel garden, you naturally head toward the two low benches on the far side, but to get there, you have to slow down, as the path is not very wide and weaves through the planting—the placement of which means you become very aware of where you tread. Self-seeded plants are dotted around and play a huge part in this part of the garden. Evening primrose (*Oenothera*) and orange poppies (*Papaver lateritium*) sort of tease in and out of the other plants, as well as a little area of wild geraniums that I let do their thing.

Then, you reach the seating, which is a wonderful area to be in at the end of the day, just as the sun's going down, with a glass of something. I've chosen plants here that have lots of lovely detail and will ensure a long season, with many having great-looking seedheads that look good right through to winter.

When you're sitting there on the low Japanese seats, it feels as if you're completely immersed in and engaged with the plants. The space also feels very comfortable to be in because there are walls on two sides, and the plants at eye level and above wrap around you. On a sunny day, you do feel you could be in another part of the world.

I'm really drawn to this idea of being enveloped by plants, as it takes me back to my childhood and that feeling of being safe and wallowing in it all. I often think back to my Scruffy Nan's garden, where you walked through the gateway and literally had to push your way through the plants, and from my viewpoint as a small child, everything felt so big. There is something quite reassuring about that for me.

The path wraps around the red-purple *Calycanthus*, while the *Phlomis* picks up the yellow of the kniphofia farther into the space.

Achillea 'Inca Gold'

Achillea 'Inca Gold'
Yarrow 'Inca Gold'

Height 28in (70cm) **Spread** 12in (30cm) **Time of flower** Summer **Soil** Most types **Position** Full sun **Hardiness** Fully hardy

The first in the list when it comes to dry garden planting, it seems to set the tone. It's a clump-forming perennial with aromatic, semi-evergreen foliage that is soft, feathery, and tactile. In my garden, it's not the longest-living plant, but that said, don't be put off, as it's easy to propagate. Stems rise from the base foliage, which are pretty sturdy and hold up well. These carry flat heads of flowers that are a softer orange/yellow with an interesting center that is nearly gray and fade to bronzy gold later in the season. It is tolerant of dry soil once it is established, and it does like a sunny spot. And on top that, it makes a nice cut flower!

Acis autumnalis 'September Snow'
Autumn snowflake

Height 6in (15cm) **Spread** 6in (15cm) **Time of flower** Late summer–fall **Soil** Well-drained **Position** Full sun/partial shade **Hardiness** Fully hardy

This is a plant that I think is well worth the wait, because in all honesty, for most of the year, it does not bring much to the game. From spring, it looks a lot like a small wiry grass, and then—bang!—in late summer and even early fall, wonderful pure white, nodding bell flowers arrive on the dark stems. The blooms come at a time of year when you just don't expect that sort of impact in the garden. My advice with this plant is to remember where you put it; otherwise, you could easily mistake it for a weedy little grass. It is a tiny bulb that I do plant in the green, and it's a real favorite.

Acis autumnalis 'September Snow'

Alchemilla caucasica
Corsican Lady's Mantle

Height 10in (25cm) **Spread** 10in (25cm) **Time of flower**
Summer **Soil** Moist but well-drained **Position** Full sun/
partial shade **Hardiness** Fully hardy

When it comes to *Alchemilla*, most gardeners know
Alchemilla mollis, which will seed around freely, is happy
in most gardens, and is a real worker, but there are
hundreds of different species of this plant. A friend gave
me this little beauty a while back, and it went straight into
my gravel garden, where it looks quite at home. Mind
you, in its country of origin—Turkey, in the Caucasus—it's
found in meadows! It is happy in sun or partial shade.
The foliage has quite a definite toothing, plus visible hairy
edges, and the flowers are a soft yellow, shaped like little
stars. It carries the same charm of its bigger cousin in the
way the leaves hold water on the surface, something that
has fascinated me since I was a kid.

Callistemon pityoides

Alpine bottlebrush

Height 5ft (1.5m) **Spread** 3ft (1m) **Time of flower** Summer **Soil** Most types **Position** Full sun/dappled shade/partial shade **Hardiness** Frost hardy/half hardy

This plant takes me back to college in Devon and is a reminder of how much our environment has changed. On a tour of the walled garden, our teacher showed us a *Callistemon* planted against a wall and pruned beautifully, telling us it was a tender plant that could only be grown with the protection and shelter of the wall, so you would think it had no chance where I live in eastern England! Well, I've been successfully growing it in the gravel garden for five or six years. *Callistemon* are Australian natives that belong to the myrtle family, and although some species are hardier than others, *Callistemon pityoides* seems to be one of the hardiest. It has a lovely upright form with firm, small, narrow leaves that are almost spiky and carry a soft citrus scent. The bottlebrush flowers are a creamy yellow, stunning from the moment they form until fully open. They hold well, to the delight of bees, making way for brown fruit that looks like hawthorn berries. It loves sun and tolerates dry conditions once established.

Crithmum maritimum

Rock samphire

Height 12in (30cm) **Spread** 12in (30cm) **Time of flower** Summer **Soil** Sand, light loam, free-draining **Position** Full sun/partial shade **Hardiness** Hardy

This plant is commonly known as rock samphire because it loves sandy dunes or a rocky spot. *Maritimum* is from the Latin, meaning "near the sea," so it's no surprise that you will often see this along the coastline in the southwest, which is where I first saw it, happily doing its thing in North Devon. I can remember one of the old boys in the Parks Department telling me it was edible, and looking into it, there is a long history of it being used in the kitchen. It is also a member of the carrot family. It is a succulent and has fleshy green-gray pinnate leaves, but upon closer look, you will see they have a triangular form. Above this, the plant carries small, creamy-green, umbrella-shaped flowers. It has quite an interesting, scrambling habit and looks great in a rock garden or, as I grow it, through a gravelly space. It does not need much in the way of nutrients and can handle salty winds, which makes it a lovely plant for a coastal garden.

Eryngium x tripartitum

Tripartite eryngo

Height 24in (60cm) **Spread** 12in (30cm) **Time of flower** Summer **Soil** Most types **Position** Full sun **Hardiness** Fully hardy

I first saw eryngiums growing along the coast when surfing in Devon, but I didn't start using them until I worked for Geoff, years later. I have tried different varieties over the years, and one of my favorite ways to use them is peppered through dry planting schemes, where they add a real architectural punch and draw the eye. Plus, it's wonderful watching small birds cleaning out the seeds through the winter months. I do like *tripartitum* as a hybrid—it seems reliable and is a little smaller than other varieties, so it works well in my gravel garden, plus eryngiums love my drier conditions. This beauty clumps up well, with base leaves that are quite leathery and have a deep green color, forming a strong base. The flower stems are wiry, and the upper part carries a blue tone that looks great with the near-electric-blue, teasel-like flowers. They have a real intensity, wrapped with delicate, lance-shaped bracts. The stems will take you well into fall, after which they brown nicely and hold form throughout the winter, so I don't tidy them up until the following February.

Euonymus nanus var. turkestanicus

Spindle

Height 3ft (1m) **Spread** 3ft (1m) **Time of flower** Spring **Soil** Moist but well-drained **Position** Full sun/partial shade **Hardiness** Fully hardy

I'm always on the lookout for a different variety of a species that I know, and this one definitely falls into that category. *Turkestanicus* is a dwarf spindle, a deciduous shrub that has an arching habit that gives it a real focal pull. The stems and leaves are slim and a rich green, turning burgundy in fall. In roughly late spring to early summer, small purplish-brown flowers are carried on the delicate stalks, which are nice enough, but it is the next stage that creates a real moment in the garden: The fruit arrives and is relatively large and pink before splitting to reveal orange seeds. This variety is more than happy in the middle of my gravel garden, where it will thrive in full sun or partial shade.

Callistemon pityoides

Eryngium x tripartitum

Crithmum maritimum

Euonymus nanus var. turkestanicus

Kniphofia 'Little Maid'
Red-hot poker 'Little Maid'

Height 24in (60cm) **Spread** 18in (45cm)
Time of flower Summer **Soil** Rich and
fertile **Position** Full sun **Hardiness**
Fully hardy

In general, *Kniphofia* are easy to grow and
can provide a real punch of color. With soft
yellows to rich reds, it's not hard to see
why it's known as the torch lily. This one
really caught my eye, first of all because of
its story. You will love this: 'Little Maid'
started as a gift in seeds from artist Cedric
Morris to Beth Chatto! I would have loved
to be present when they chatted about
plants. You can see why it has become so
popular, as it feels like a tasteful little plant.
First of all, its flower is a little softer than so
many other red-hot pokers, as it is a lemon
yellow that softens as the season moves
on, flowering from midsummer right
through to late fall. It has neat, slim, and
compact growth that provides really good
variety. It loves a little sun and is not overly
fussy in terms of soil—just avoid anything
really wet in the winter. It will tolerate
drought and cuts well for display indoors.

Limonium platyphyllum
Broad-leaved statice

Height 24in (60cm) **Spread** 22in (55cm)
Time of flower Summer **Soil** Well-drained
to dry **Position** Full sun **Hardiness**
Fully hardy

I first saw *Limonium* on a Greek Island,
growing en masse in full flower on a
rough piece of ground not far from the
sea. It was like looking at clouds from
above, so as you can imagine, as soon
as I came back, I found *Limonium
platyphyllum* and have been growing it
ever since. It suits my dry conditions,
plus every time I look at it, it reminds me
of the sea. It's a herbaceous perennial
that flowers in midsummer; provides
masses of tiny, single, soft, lavender-blue
flowers that are carried on straight wiry
stems; and is attractive to pollinating
insects. The whole look is paper-like, and
that lasts as they dry, which makes them
great for cutting and drying. Later in the
season, each flower capsule carries a
single seed above evergreen basal leaves
that are broad, ovate-shaped, and leathery
to the touch, with a waved detail at the
edge. They really look at home in the
gravel garden.

Muehlenbeckia astonii
Wiggy-wig bush

Height 6½ft (2m) **Spread** 5–6½ft (1.5–2m)
Time of flower Summer **Soil** Most types
Position Full sun/partial shade **Hardiness**
Fully hardy

This wacky plant from New Zealand is
an unusual shrub that will always draw
comments (my kids loved it when they
first saw it), and it has the coolest of
common names: It's known as the "wiggy
wig bush," which I loved saying on
TV (I am still a little boy at heart)! It's an
arty-looking plant; in the winter, it's a mass
of thin, brown, wire mesh that has been
twisted and molded, and after rain, it just
looks magical. It's hard to believe a plant
can grow that way. Tiny, green, heart-
shaped leaves with a lovely soft sheen
cover the shrub. Small white flowers
appear in the summer. You may read
it only handles 23°F (-5°C), but in my dry
soil, it has survived a lot more. I have seen
this plant clipped into some wonderful
shapes over the years; it looks great as
clipped mounds or repeated forms
through gravel planting. It makes a good
coastal plant, as it's happy in sun or partial
shade and enjoys well-drained soil.

Pratia pedunculata
Blue star creeper

Height 2in (5cm) **Spread** Indefinite **Time
of flower** Summer **Soil** Moisture-retentive
Position Full sun/partial shade **Hardiness**
Fully hardy

This is a dainty little thing and a lot hardier
than it looks. It is related to *Campanula*,
and when you see it in bloom, you'll
understand why. It's another plant that I
first saw while working for Geoff, where it
was happily growing in a little alpine
garden. It has tiny, soft green leaves that
are lovely to the touch—they feel a little
spongy. It really hugs the ground as it
grows, matting up quickly, but it is not at all
invasive. Over the years, I have used it a lot
between large gaps in paving, around
stepping-stones, and as groundcover in
smaller gardens. In late spring and early
summer, the plant can be covered in a
mass of sky-blue, star-shaped flowers with
darker central veins; they really are the
color of a perfect summer day. It does well
planted in wok-style containers, as it has a
very shallow root system.

GRAVEL GARDEN

Veronica gentianoides
Gentian speedwell

Height 20in (50cm) **Spread** 8in (20cm) **Time of flower** Spring–summer **Soil** Most types **Position** Full sun/partial shade **Hardiness** Fully hardy

Veronica is a huge genus with around 500 species, and I can perfectly remember the first time I saw this particular one: I was doing a little weeding in a small alpine garden in my early days working at Barnsdale, and I could see the sky-blue spires of flowers gently moving in a slightly hypnotic way. I can remember thinking how cool and graceful they were. I have been growing it ever since—not just for the flowers, which appear in early summer and carry a subtle veining, but because it also forms a good carpet of dark glossy-green leaves that cover the ground and seem able to handle my drier conditions. This plant works really well in the gravel garden, and it benefits from being divided every few years to keep everything looking fresh. All in all, this is an enchanting little speedwell.

Sedum aizoon 'Euphorbioides'
Aizoon stonecrop 'Euphorbioides'

Height 12in (30cm) **Spread** 12in (30cm) **Time of flower** Summer **Soil** Light, well-drained **Position** Full sun **Hardiness** Fully hardy

This plant's common name of "stonecrop" pretty well tells you where it loves to grow. In the wild, it is found on grassy slopes and rocky spots, so it really suits the well-drained, drier conditions of a gravel garden. It prefers full sun but can handle partial shade as long as it has good drainage. Its compact growth makes it good for small spaces, and it has a lovely, mounded, clump-forming habit. Stems are stout and a rich red, dressed with lance-shaped, fleshy green leaves that have a real sheen and feel quite vibrant. It also has a strong shape and looks great in and around vertical plants. Then, around June, rich bronze flower buds open out into warm yellow-orange clusters of star-shaped flowers that keep going well into fall and pull in the pollinators. The play between leaf, flower, and stem is really interesting on this plant, and I think this cultivar is particularly striking and maybe a little underused.

Veronica gentianoides

129

UPPER COURTYARD AND GREENHOUSE

Off the gravel garden in a small courtyard sits the greenhouse. The space works well, tucked away and hidden by a hawthorn hedge and underplanted with shade-loving plants. This is where I go if I just want to be alone with my thoughts.

I think sometimes in our gardens we can be a little quick to slash and burn. What I mean by that is we can rip things out without proper thought. When we moved in here, the hawthorn hedge was very overgrown, and you had to fight your way through to get to the greenhouse area, and then when you got there, it felt a little claustrophobic. The easiest thing to do would have been to rip out the hedge and free up the central space, but in doing that, I would have lost some of the screening. The bottom of the hedge was not great. I could, of course, have taken it back to the ground, and it being hawthorn, it would have grown back, but it would have taken some time. We gardeners can be a little fearful of pruning, but most often, with a little research and confidence, you'll be fine. I have used pruners, loppers, and even a pruning saw when needed to take all the lower horizontal growths back to the main stems, making sure I was working as closely to the vertical stem as possible.

This opened up the space to access the greenhouse, which is an important element in my garden. Where I live it gets very cold, and helping plants thrive can be a bit hit or miss. My greenhouse is relatively small, with limited space, so I have to be selective about which plants can be kept there during the winter. It is also unheated, so some years, I may add fleece around the plants if it is particularly frosty. If I lose a few things, I simply won't try them again, and I see it as an opportunity to try something new the following year—particularly tougher plants that will survive even in an unheated greenhouse.

Planting Plan

Perennials

- *Disporum longistylum* 'Night Heron'
- *Epimedium* 'Valor'
- *Geranium phaeum* 'Lilacina'
- *Gymnocarpium dryopteris*
- *Maianthemum bifolium*
- *Paris quadrifolia*
- *Polygonatum orientale*
- *Polystichum polyblepharum*
- *Polystichum setiferum* (Divisilobum Group) 'Herrenhausen'

Bulbs

Allium ursinum

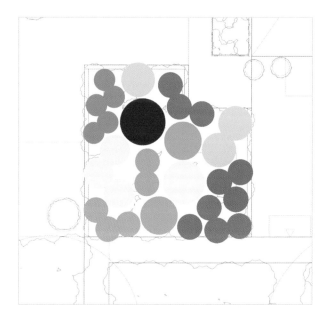

Underplanting the
hawthorn hedge
once I had lifted
the canopy.

Underplanting the hedge

The way a bed is going to be viewed really drives the way you put things together, meaning detail can play a major part in the planning stage. In my garden, this is a little area that will mostly be viewed from above and when perched in the greenhouse courtyard with a cup of tea, so I wanted it to feel like a wild hedgerow.

Once I had raised the hedge canopy, I improved the soil by forking through a 4in (10cm) layer of well-rotted horse manure, avoiding the roots of the hedge and not raising the soil level around the stems. If you like, you can repeat this mulching over subsequent years, as it is not just the hedge that will make demands on your soil.

When it comes to choosing the plants, because a lot of the woodland plants sing their loudest during early spring, and I wanted this area to carry interest throughout the year,

I was drawn to ferns that set a textural tone but also provided me with the bones to develop the rest of the scene. Here, the flowers will come and go, so varying greens, leaf shapes, and finishes play a big part. The differences don't always have to be huge—even a subtle variation can be enough to draw your interest.

From this, I added a few plants that would provide groundcover over time, but I did not need deep soil to root well. Finally, I added taller plants that might need a little more depth of soil. I know this is not how everyone would put the area together, but you need to adapt depending on your conditions and what you are trying to achieve, and creating some groundcover here was very important.

From left to right: Raising the canopy using pruners, using a hand rake to clear away cuttings, spreading out compost, designing the plant layout, and watering after planting.

The raised canopy hedge is now being treated as a pleached hedge, which is maintained by clipping twice a year.

Disporum longistylum '**Night Heron**'

Long-styled disporum 'Night Heron'

Height 3–4ft (90–120cm) **Spread** 12in (30cm) **Time of flower** Summer **Soil** Moist but well-drained **Position** Partial shade **Hardiness** Fully hardy

You will see variations in this plant, so do buy it in the flesh. Once it gets going, you will have yourself a little drama—in a good way. Popping up among ferns and other larger-leafed woodland plants, it looks fantastic. The stems are dark—nearly black in some cases—and carry lightly spread, rich glossy-green leaves alternately that turn a dark-olive green as we move through the year. Creamy green, small, bell-shaped flowers arrive in late spring in clusters, when the stems start to arch. But the display does not stop there! Dark purple berries follow, which last very much into winter. This is an elegant plant that will clump in time, and I don't tend to cut out last year's foliage until a little later into the new season, as it provides support for the new growth. The farther away from shade I have grown it, I've found the more moisture it needs.

Epimedium '**Valor**'

Epimedium 'Valor'

Height 12in (30cm) **Spread** 12in (30cm) **Time of flower** Spring **Soil** Most types **Position** Sun/partial shade **Hardiness** Fully hardy

This little beauty is a hybrid of *Epimedium wushanense* and *Epimedium perralderianum*. I do think epimediums are a little underrated—well, definitely by Mrs. Frost! I have them popping up across the garden, where they provide great fall color, as they can be evergreen or deciduous. There are more than thirty different species, so you will find one that works in sun or shade. They are long-lived plants that bear wonderful, delicate flowers that are a creamy white with yellow centers. The new foliage of *Epimedium* 'Valor' has a rusty finish to the tips and serrated edges, which as the season moves on turn green with a shine. I also use these plants in pots, where they work well. They do seem to be the sort of plant that you will soon find yourself getting more of until you have yourself quite a little collection—like me!

Geranium phaeum 'Lilacina'
Dusky cranesbill 'Lilacina'

Height 28in (70cm) **Spread** 16in (40m) **Time of flower** Summer **Soil** Any good, garden soil, just not too damp **Position** Sun/partial shade/full shade **Hardiness** Fully hardy

Geranium phaeum is a hard-working, valuable member of a group I call "get-out-of-jail" plants! It has never let me down, and over the years I have sought out different varieties. The plant has handsome foliage that varies in color, depending on the variety. It will endure a hard cutback if it becomes a little untidy, then a few weeks later, you'll have a mound of fresh growth that will carry through the rest of the year. *Geranium phaeum* 'Lilacina' bears delicate lilac flowers with a distinct white center. The foliage feels quite open and divided. It has a matte finish and is a mid-green early in the year, darkening as the season goes on. Like other *Geranium phaeum*, it's happy in reasonably good garden soil—it just doesn't like it very wet. I grow my plants in shade, partial shade, and even sunnier spots in good soil.

Gymnocarpium dryopteris
Oak fern

Height 8in (20cm) **Spread** 16in (40cm) **Time of flower** N/A **Soil** Moist but well-drained **Position** Dappled shade/partial shade/full shade **Hardiness** Hardy

If I could only ever have one fern, this would be the one. It's not big, fancy, or flashy, but I love its delicate appearance. It is a robust, native little thing that in time will provide a stunning carpet. Once it has its roots in, its rhizomes will start to roam, which just adds to its charm. I have seen this plant in the wild, and en masse it looks incredible. It's commonly called the oak fern. The thin, dark, wire-like stems create layers of leaves like a little canopy, giving the effect of a mini woodland, and its green color is the celebration of spring. So fresh. For me, it works well in dappled and full shade, but I always make sure the soil is as rich as possible, as I do feel it likes a little moisture to get going. It would also benefit from a little mulch of leaf mold each year.

Maianthemum bifolium
Two-leaved false lily of the valley

Height 8in (20cm) **Spread** 3ft (1m) **Time of flower** Summer **Soil** Moist but well-drained **Position** Partial shade/full shade **Hardiness** Fully hardy

Maianthemum is a widespread genus and another American relative of Solomon's seal. It's a very pretty, low-growing, creeping plant that spreads quite slowly via rhizomes to eventually form a good, mat-like carpet. For a small plant, the leaves are a good size and heart-like in shape. It looks a little like lily of the valley, with its white clusters of flowers followed by red berries that last through the summer. Mine seem to need a little early moisture and then tend to be fine for the rest of the year, so if we do have a dry spring, I keep an eye on it. It is a very hardy plant that looks super as it creeps under taller plants.

Paris quadrifolia
Four-leaved grass

Height 12–16in (30–40cm) **Spread** 6–18in (15–45cm) **Time of flower** Summer **Soil** Most types **Position** Full sun/partial shade/full shade **Hardiness** Hardy

Paris is not the largest genus, and interestingly, it is related to *Trillium*—when you see the two together, the similarities are there. It's a plant I came across a good ten or so years ago, and if I'm honest, I'm still experimenting with it. It is a plant that I will buy in bloom if I can. It looks a little exotic; the leaves remind me of a tongue, with normally four protruding from a central stem, but I have seen five or six on one stem! Each stem carries a single star-like flower, whose underside is green with almost white upper petals. At the tips it produces a rich, black berry, which birds enjoy eating. Given the chance, this berry will ripen to reveal bright red seeds, and if you want to collect them, make sure you protect the plants in drier years—I mulch well after a good soaking. The plants may retreat early, but they will reappear the following spring. Also, you may see the label say it needs an acidic soil, but with a little TLC, it does well for me. You may even find it on a woodland walk.

Paris quadrifolia

Polygonatum orientale
Tall persicaria

Height 16in (40cm) **Spread** 12in (30cm) **Time of flower** Late spring–summer **Soil** Most types **Position** Partial shade **Hardiness** Hardy

Polygonatum comes from the ancient Greek for "many knees," which references the joints on the creeping rhizomes. It's a large family of plants, and we do have a few that are native, but others can be found across Europe to Asia. It hails from the Asparagaceae family, which you can see with the berries it produces after the flowers. It is an excellent Solomon's seal, which was a plant that fascinated me as a kid, as my Scruffy Nan used to have it popping up all over her garden. The good news is that this variety does not seem to be susceptible to Solomon's seal sawfly. The leaves are lush and deeply veined and alternate up the stem, and its arching habit really helps show off its flowers, which hang in couples and are white and bell-shaped, with a green tinge to them. It's happy in partial shade, but I do work some organic matter into the soil before planting.

Polygonatum orientale

Polystichum setiferum (Divisilobum Group) 'Herrenhausen'

Polystichum setiferum (Divisilobum Group) 'Herrenhausen'
Soft shield fern 'Herrenhausen'

Height 3ft (1m) **Spread** 2½–3ft (80–100cm) **Time of flower** N/A **Soil** Moist but well-drained **Position** Partial shade/full shade **Hardiness** Fully hardy

Shield ferns are another go-to for me. There are around 200 species across the world, and I think they are one of the best garden ferns, with a real grace. One of the things I love about them is the spore pattern under the leaves—it's stunning! *Polystichum setiferum* is probably one of our loveliest native ferns: The evergreen fronds are a light, nearly golden green, unfurling as the season moves forward and darkening as they mature, with a matte finish. When designing garden plans, this option really helps, because they contrast so well with other shade-loving plants. I do like using 'Herrenhausen' to drive the woodland floor, setting these first, then contrasting other plants with them. In larger areas, they look good in random drifts through a woodland setting. As the fronds unfurl in spring, I tend to go in with the pruners and tidy up older leaves, which helps you enjoy the new growth, but don't go too crazy!

UPPER TERRACE WRAP

The upper terrace wrap is the final section of my garden. It's an odd shape, a bit like a wedge of cheese, with two straight sides and a curve. The woodland starts at the rear of the garden and wraps around the courtyard, providing a backdrop to the main terrace and enclosing the gravel garden, where the planting provides privacy and screening, making it feel secluded.

My starting points in this little space were the deep hawthorn hedge and two old, quirky-looking medlars (*Mespilus germanica*). I liked the idea of having a calm, green backdrop for the gravel garden, so it seemed natural that this spot would make a nice little woodland area. It was a bit of an awkward corner, which wasn't easy to access, so I repeated a tiny bark pathway, which adds to the woodland atmosphere and helps carry the eye. This little path leaves the greenhouse and travels along the back boundary, wrapping around to the rear of the gravel garden.

The medlars sat like two big old lumps, so I lifted their canopies by about 5ft (1.5m) to open up the space and let in more light and air. Medlars are quite odd in that they grow in all sorts of weird directions, so lifting the canopy means you get to see the gnarly and sculptural stem patterns. They also have a long season of interest, with soft, furry foliage emerging in spring, followed by beautiful white flowers and unusual-looking fruit in fall. It also has fantastic fall color.

As in the upper courtyard, I did the same shaping with the hawthorn, which runs along the boundaries; pleached hawthorn is not something you see very often, but as well as making the area feel lighter and more interesting, it gives me an extra 3ft (1m) of bed beneath the trees.

Woodland trees and shrubs

I planted a multi-stem rowan (*Sorbus aucuparia*) and cornelian cherry (*Cornus mas*) in this woodland space, the latter of which is a slightly different variety than the one in the lower part of the garden, but it brings a sense of

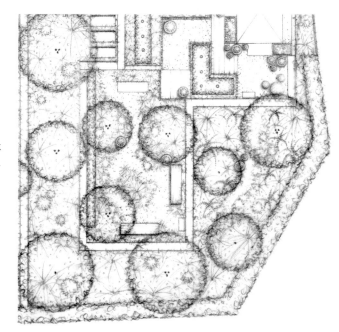

Woodland wrap

continuity and adds a vertical element alongside the two medlars. Both bring seasonal interest and also connect the garden with the surrounding area, including the trees at the end of the neighbor's garden, and those on the terrace that lead the eye to a huge ash tree in a field about 98–131ft (30–40m) away. The trees have also helped provide a bit of natural privacy screening from the houses positioned above ours.

The seasonal change of medlar trees is a real spectacle. The russet-brown fruits ripen in fall and the foliage takes on fiery, orangey tones.

Cercidiphyllum japonicum
Katsura tree

Height 40–50ft (12–15m) **Spread** 16–26ft (5–8m) **Time of flower** Spring **Soil** Fertile but well-drained **Position** Full sun/partial shade **Hardiness** Fully hardy

I could not talk about trees without mentioning this plant. The first year I worked at Barnsdale, on a frosty fall morning, I was wandering around the garden, and halfway up, I could smell what I thought was toffee. I eventually figured out it was coming from the frosted leaves of the *Cercidiphyllum* and discovered that's why it is also known as the "cotton candy tree." Over the years, I have lost count of how many I have planted. If I'm working for a client who has kids, they normally get one, as I like the idea of them trying to figure out where that smell is coming from! In fall, the leaves become yellow, red, orange, and even pink. It can reach 50ft (15m) in time, but growing it as a multi-stem will restrict the growth a little. Be mindful that the early leaves can get caught by late frost, but they do come back. All in all, it's a very elegant deciduous tree.

Cornus mas
Cornelian cherry

Height 8–13ft (2.5–4m) **Spread** 8–13ft (2.5–4m) **Time of flower** Winter **Soil** Moist but well-drained **Position** Full sun/partial shade **Hardiness** Hardy

This is one of my favorite small trees, because it's full of character and is a plant that just keeps giving. In late winter, it can become a real star, when the bare branches become covered with bright yellow flowers and are followed by red cherry-like fruit. It's a compact tree that I tend to grow as a multi-stem, and as it matures, the bark begins to peel and reveal copper tones. *Cornus mas* is native to central and southern Europe and will not ask a lot of you, as it's pretty tough, tolerates most soils and conditions, and will take 10–20 years to reach maturity, plus it responds well to pruning. I have clipped the top of mine in the garden to create lovely domed shapes. I have seen them pleached as well as a great standard tree.

Euonymus europaeus 'Red Cascade'
Spindle 'Red Cascade'

Height 10–13ft (3–4m) **Spread** 3–6½ft (1–2m) **Time of flower** Summer **Soil** Moist but well-drained **Position** Full sun/partial shade **Hardiness** Fully hardy

Euonymus is a versatile genus, including everything from evergreen and deciduous shrubs to small trees like this one, which is known for its stunning fall display. But I think it brings a lot more to the party than that! It's a quite light, airy tree, and in early spring, the ovate, soft-sheened bright-green leaves emerge, which mellow as the season moves on. Come May to early June, it produces small yellow flowers that give way to a red-pink fruit with orange seed cases. Sounds strange, I know, but the contrast of foliage and stem works! In late September, the leaves turn a rich vibrant red, and the whole scene comes together, carried into the winter. It looks incredible. I tend to grow this as a multi-stem so I can keep it contained, but I have also seen it sold as a standard and larger shrub. It's a tough tree that works well in most soils—even my limey soil—and the only place I have seen it struggle is in very wet conditions.

Helwingia chinensis
Chinese helwingia

Height 4ft (1.2m) **Spread** 5ft (1.5m) **Time of flower** Spring **Soil** Most types **Position** Partial shade **Hardiness** Fully hardy

Once you see this plant in bloom, you will never forget it—not because they are the most stunning but because of where they appear! The flower is tiny in proportion to the shrub and is located on the central vein of the leaf, with a red-purple bud opening into a purple-green flower in summer. On female plants, this is followed by a cherry-red, pea-shaped fruit. All in all, it's a little crazy; plants never cease to amaze me. The new growth starts out a lovely brown with a copper undertone that gives it a really warm feel, then it turns green as the year moves on. The leaves are semi-evergreen and lanceolate in shape, a little willow-like with a soft leathery finish, carrying a scarcely serrated edge. I tend to grow this in a sheltered spot in semi-shade. I really like its relaxed, mounding growth habit, which makes it very easy to plant, especially alongside more textured plants.

Cercidiphyllum japonicum

Euonymus europaeus 'Red Cascade'

Cornus mas

Helwingia chinensis

141

Mespilus germanica
Common medlar

Height 10ft (3m) **Spread** 10ft (3m) **Time of flower** Spring
Soil Moist but well-drained **Position** Full sun **Hardiness**
Hardy (with some protection from frost)

We had a medlar in our garden when I was a kid. It was a
great tree to climb when we used to play war, as the fruit
made the best bullets. I wonder if the Romans used them!
I know they saw them as quite a delicacy. Medlars even
get a few lines in *Romeo and Juliet*:

"Mercutio
If love be blind, love cannot hit the mark.
Now will he sit under a medlar tree,"

I love the fact that Shakespeare must have looked at this
tree and thought, "What can I say about this?" and then
worked it into his love story! The medlar is a small,
wide-spreading tree with large, russet-brown, unusual-
shaped fruit. These are not everyone's cup of tea and
should not be eaten raw, but left to partially decay, the
flavor changes. I grow medlars not for their fruit but as a
great garden tree, usually as a standard or multi-stem. In
early spring, the green leaves emerge with a matte finish
and soft to the touch, then in later spring, a mass of large
white flowers arrives, which looks lovely. In fall, the famous
fruits ripen, and the leaves turn bright yellow. It can be
easily pruned and shaped and will live for a long time.

Mespilus germanica

Sambucus nigra f. *porphyrophylla* 'Thundercloud'

Sambucus nigra f. porphyrophylla 'Thundercloud'
Elder 'Thundercloud'

Height 8–13ft (2.5–4m) **Spread** 5–8ft (1.5–2.5m) **Time of
flower** Summer **Soil** Moist but well-drained **Position** Full
sun/partial shade **Hardiness** Hardy

By all accounts, the elder is feared by the devil, but it
is a plant that has been well-neutralized by our forebears.
It has been very useful over the years for both food
and dye—and the hollow stems were even used by
the Saxons for blowing air to help get a fire going. I do
love seeing people out picking elder flowers and
berries in hedgerows in the summer, as I think that simple
connection to the past is really special. Over the years,
I have seen more varieties come to market, but if I am
honest, some feel a little overbred—but who am I to say?
For me, 'Thundercloud' seems to strike a good balance
between having the looks of the famous elder figure and
drawing us through the seasons. In spring, divided

Sorbus aucuparia
Rowan

Height 26–33ft (8–10m) **Spread** 13–26ft (4–8m) **Time of flower** Spring **Soil** Well-drained **Position** Full sun/partial shade **Hardiness** Fully hardy

If you want to keep evil spirits at bay, by all accounts, you need a rowan in your life! This is one of my favorite native trees and a super garden tree. The first thing that caught my eye is the leaves, which are nearly fern-like but also have a lovely blue-green tone underneath. In spring, clusters of creamy-white flowers contrast well with this foliage, and then come fall, the leaves turn a mix of orange to golden yellow. The flowers are followed by orange-red berries that are doing their thing by September. It's a great tree for wildlife, too; the flowers provide pollen and nectar for pollinators, and the berries offer food for birds. It's another tree I grow as a multi-stem, as it has a wonderful smooth bark that ages to tones of gray and bronze and a rougher texture. It's happy in most soils, except those that are very heavy, but I normally look for a cooler spot in the garden.

palmate leaves start off burgundy and become a richer, almost black color as the season goes on. This makes a great foil for the flowers, which start as red buds and open into flattened panicles of fragrant pink and white heads, before giving way to dark, nearly black glossy berries—which, if you don't use, will be enjoyed by the birds. I have grown 'Thundercloud' for a good while now, and it is a strong grower, and if it's left for 5–10 years, it will make a small tree. But don't let that put you off if you have a smaller space, as it does stool well—I tend to do this in the spring to drive the richness of the foliage. It will grow in most soils and is happy in sun or partial shade. 'Thundercloud' is as happy in a small garden as it is in an ornamental border—whether you prefer making wine or cordial from the flowers or using the vitamin-rich berries for jams or other dishes.

Sorbus aucuparia

Woodland planting

I wanted to ensure seasonal interest in this part of the garden but also have fun with woodland plants. As ever with the herbaceous layer, it's about playing with texture, shape, and form. I like the way the lower planting creates a cloud-like, billowy effect.

However, the layers are not just for me but also a way of creating an important habitat for wildlife by providing food in the form of berries and seeds and creating safety for creatures working their way down to the ground.

There was already some wood spurge (*Euphorbia amygdaloides* var. *robbiae*) scrambling back under the hedge that worked well, so I left that in place, and now the plants form a little evergreen wave through the back of this border. Here, I've added lots of other shade-loving plants, such as epimediums, *Geranium phaeum*, ferns, and disporum.

Colin at my local nursery, Swines Meadow, is obsessed with woodland plants, and I've gotten all sorts of goodies from him, including a shade-loving form of *Lysimachia* (*L. paridiformis* var. *stenophylla*) collected by the great plantsman Roy Lancaster. Every time I look at that plant, I don't just think, "That's a nice plant"—I remember that Roy, one of my great gardening heroes, found it and thought it worthy of bringing back from one of his plant-hunting

expeditions. And now I have it in my garden! For me, that makes this plant even more magical. Someone collected it, someone else propagated it, then I went and bought it and brought it home to care for it. That in itself is a wonderful thing.

I feel so lucky when it comes to plants, knowing that there are lots of people as infatuated with them as I am! I know that I am not alone in my obsessions, because I can just go to a nursery or talk to people at garden shows and find like-minded souls. I find that even the quietest people in the world come alive when they start talking about their favorite plants.

Woodland plants tend to create an atmosphere of softness, calm, and coolness. To me, they seem to say, "Just come in, sit down, and let's have a quiet moment," and because this little area is at the end of the garden, it has become a place we escape to. So, I've put in a little bistro table and chairs, and it's the perfect place to hide yourself away where nobody can see you. It's got a different feeling than the Heligan-esque woodland planting of the courtyard; it's more eclectic and feels a little more hunter-driven. It's another example of how the design process for this new garden in some spaces was a reaction to what was already there and to gently improve the area.

Allium ursinum
Wild garlic

Height 12in (30cm) **Spread** 3ft (1m) **Time of flower**
Spring–summer **Soil** Moist but well-drained **Position**
Partial shade/shade **Hardiness** Fully hardy

These little bulbs take me back to the first spring when
I lived in Devon; there was a woodland close by, and the
air was filled with the aroma of garlic. Yes, I had seen
these bulbs before, but never in this number. I loved
it—not just the smell, but the green carpet punctuated
with stunning white flowers was one of the most
beautiful things I had seen. In Devon, it is referred to
as "cows' leek," as cows love it. By all accounts, it can help
purify blood and reduce cholesterol, and I do wonder
sometimes if the cows figured that out! It self-seeds and
has creeping rhizomes, which means it can create good
groundcover. It does like fertile soil, and I have seen it in
damper spots, but it also works well in my drier soil—you
might read that it prefers acidic soil, but I don't seem to
have any problems growing it. The leaves and flowers can
be eaten and carry a mild garlic flavor, which is great in so
many dishes—soups and, possibly my favorite, pesto—
and I think it should be celebrated more than it is. It is
best to pick it earlier in the season, in late spring.

Allium ursinum

Aralia californica
Elk clover

Height 6½ft (2m) **Spread** 3ft (1m) **Time of flower** Summer
Soil Moderately humus-rich **Position** Full sun/partial
shade **Hardiness** Hardy

In California, where this plant is native, it is known as elk
clover. It's a gem of a plant, a large, strong, architectural
perennial, but it does blow my mind how much growth
this plant will get in a year, once it gets its roots in and
starts to establish itself. The woody stems are hairy and
covered with bright green pinnate leaves. Late in the
summer, elegant sprays of white flowers appear, which
are followed by attractive, dark, globose berries in fall,
when the whole plant turns a buttery golden yellow. The
advice is usually to plant in acidic soil, but it does fine in
my alkaline soil—although I do work in a lot of composted
bark before planting. It's a plant that will make a real
statement in a woodland scheme, and while it is tolerant
of sun or partial shade, if you are going to grow it in the
sun, the soil will need to carry more moisture and will
benefit from mulch to make it humus-rich.

Disporopsis pernyi

Aralia californica

Disporopsis pernyi
Perny disporopsis

Height 16in (40cm) **Spread** 16in (40cm) **Time of flower**
Spring–summer **Soil** Rich and fertile **Position** Partial
shade/shade **Hardiness** Hardy

Not unlike the *Disporum*, this lovely, semi-evergreen
perennial is found in the mountain woodlands of China
and looks very similar to Solomon's seal, to which it is
closely related. The arching, leafy stems carry pairs of
lance-shaped leaves that are dark green and have a glossy
finish. The pendulum flowers are white with green tips
and are lemon-scented. It will happily tolerate the drier
conditions in my garden once it is established, after which
it slowly starts to spread.

147

Euphorbia amygdaloides var. *robbiae*
Mrs. Robb's bonnet

Height 24in (60cm) **Spread** 3ft (1m) **Time of flower**
Spring–summer **Soil** Most types **Position** Sun/full shade/
partial shade **Hardiness** Hardy

This is one to have in your back pocket if you need
some help to deal with that tricky spot, as it will work
hard for you, especially in dry shade. It sends out roots
underground to create a strong, deep-green mat. The
leaves have a leathery finish, then, come early spring,
lime-green, cup-shaped bracts push up through the
foliage and last well into summer. In a deeply shaded spot,
they really do sing, and I have used them to great effect in
woodland settings. Every couple of years, I go over it with
a hedge trimmer just above ground level and give the
area a good cleanup—but do wear protective clothing, as
the sap can irritate the skin. When using this plant, do not
give the soil too much care, because then the plant can
get away from you a little.

Lysimachia paridiformis var. stenophylla 'Roy Lancaster's Form'

Height 12in (30cm) **Spread** 22in (55cm) **Time of flower**
Summer **Soil** Moist but well-drained **Position** Shade/
partial shade **Hardiness** Hardy

"You will love this, Roy Lancaster collected it," I was told—I
was hooked, and I had not even seen the plant! Roy is a
man whom I have alway held in high regard; he is a
walking encyclopedia. The plant is a winner, and not what
you expect for a *Lysimachia*—it clumps and covers the
ground well. Its growth habit reminds me of *Euphorbia
robbiae*, but it really is not invasive. It looks a little like a
mini woodland, with stems carrying individual rosettes of
narrow, lance-like foliage—you could say "willow-like." The
leaves have a silky-glossy finish, and I think the plant is
worth growing for that alone, as it feels shrub-like. Come
midsummer, flowers emerge from the center of each
rosette in a form of small clusters, golden yellow in color.
The plant loves the shade, but I'd still prep the soil well to
make sure it will hold a little moisture and is not too dry.

Podophyllum peltatum

Lysimachia paridiformis var. stenophylla 'Roy Lancaster's Form'

Podophyllum peltatum
Mayapple

Height 16in (40cm) **Spread** 22in (55cm) **Time of flower**
Spring **Soil** Moist but well-drained **Position** Shade/partial
shade **Hardiness** Hardy

This is a fun plant that I first found when I was creating
an ornamental vegetable garden at the RHS Chelsea
Flower Show. It's known as the Mayapple because it
has an edible fruit that is produced after flowering in
spring—but all other parts are highly poisonous! It's
fascinating to watch grow, as it is rhizome-driven, and its
entrance is somewhat dramatic. I always feel it's erupting
from the ground, rising up like a closed umbrella that
slowly opens. Each plant will only have one or two leaves,
which are palmate in shape, quite fleshy, and mid-green in
color, with a sheen to them. While the leaves opening
blows my mind, a little later in spring, under the leaf, a
pure white nodding flower with bright yellow anthers
arrives, which you nearly have to drop to your knees to
view, as it sits hidden away. As the flower dies, a green
fleshy fruit appears that ripens to a golden yellow, which
can be used to make preserves. The plant is native to
deciduous woodlands in North America, shady fields, or
riverbanks, so it deals well with damper, drier conditions.

Polygonatum verticillatum 'Rubrum'
Whorled Solomon's seal 'Rubrum'

Height 35in (90cm) **Spread** 12in (30cm) **Time of flower** Summer **Soil** Fertile, humus-rich, moist but well-drained **Position** Shade/partial shade **Hardiness** Fully hardy

This variety makes a nice change from what we think of as the standard Solomon's seal, and I think it is an elegant addition to the species. It has tall upright stems that carry thin, almost willow-like leaves in sets of four at quite even intervals, all the way up the stem. They remind me of the quarter-hour on a clock. From these leaf axils in May/June appear small, tubular, nodding, pale pink/purple flowers, which are followed by reddy-pink berries that can last until late in the year. It's happy even in deep shade—although in that situation, it will need a little moisture. I grow my plants in a well-mulched area—think woodland! It is a lovely plant to grow up through lower textual planting.

Polystichum neolobatum

Polygonatum verticillatum 'Rubrum'

Polystichum neolobatum
Asian Saber Fern

Height 20–24in (50–60cm) **Spread** 24–31in (60–80cm) **Time of flower** N/A **Soil** Moist, fertile **Position** Dappled/full shade **Hardiness** Hardy

This is one tough fern from the Himalayas, and I have found that it deals well with drought once it gets its roots in. I have mine next to a path so I see it every day, and it just seems to look good throughout the year! The leaves have a glossy, leathery finish with undersides that are quite pale, carrying rusty brown scales that are not soft to the touch. The stems are quite wiry and interesting, unlike a lot of other ferns, with fronds that are well-divided and really do look like a series of daggers—hence the common name of "Asian saber fern." Happy in dappled or heavy shade, it can also be grown very successfully in a container, provided it is placed in a shady position.

Ranunculus aconitifolius
Fair maids of France/aconite buttercup

Height 35in (90cm) **Spread** 16in (40cm) **Time of flower** Spring–summer **Soil** Moisture-retentive **Position** Sun/partial shade **Hardiness** Hardy

I do love a buttercup. My nan was the first person to put a wild buttercup under my chin, which is a lovely memory. This variety is rather large and a real dazzler; while there are a few forms we might run from, this is not one. It is said to have originated in France—hence the common name of "fair maids of France." The first thing to say about this plant is it clumps nicely but is not invasive. In early spring, red-dusted stems carry deeply divided dark-green leaves. There is a real depth to the color, which works so well with softer-leaved plants—it looks superb interplanted with ferns. It is happy in sun or partial shade and loves a little moisture in the soil, so I prep and mulch well before planting, as I live in a drier part of the country. The "dazzler" part comes in late spring, when the stem carries a very simple, pure white, buttercup-shaped flower with a bright yellow center that really pops. One thing to be mindful of with this plant is it may retreat to the ground in the summer, but don't worry—it will reappear next year.

MOVING THROUGH THE GARDEN

"Warm Love"—Van Morrison

Moving through the garden is something many of us take for granted, but for a lot of us, it links different spaces and atmospheres, and it's probably collectively how I wanted the garden to feel. This is "Warm Love."

The layout of my garden is really simple, designed around lots of clean, strong lines. The older and more experienced I get, the simpler my approach has become. I like using just a few quality materials, such as nice timber and stone, and making sure it's all beautifully crafted and the various elements knit together nicely.

For me, it's important that a garden feels as if it belongs to the location it's in and ties in with the materials used to build the house. Getting the hard landscaping and planting right helps how you direct movement around the garden. I've used focal points and such features as sculptures, seating, arches, and pots—which I think of as commas and full stops—to draw visitors through the garden, so that as you move from space to space, you come across different viewpoints, settings, and changes of atmosphere. All these play their part in creating the garden; I wanted to people to feel comfortable in it and want to be in it.

I've put in a couple of new gates, which can also be focal points. Made of wood and nicely detailed, they are charming in their own right. An entrance gate can set a tone; it is the front door to your garden.

Climate change, the unpredictability of the weather, and the increase in pests and diseases are having a huge impact on the growing world, so I keep hard landscaping simple, but I have fun with the plants. I use a system of layering plants that includes trees, shrubs, herbaceous perennials, bulbs, and the more ephemeral annuals/biannual plants. A garden always benefits from having plants from each of these groups. In a way, this layering is a bit like how I've terraced in the garden.

The overall effect of the layout—including the terracing and the planting that softens it and helps guide the eye—is that you really can't see the extent of the garden from the front gate or back door. As you enter the garden, the story starts to unfold; the eye is led along the pathway, steps, planting, pots, and the various features, but there's not really a point where you know what's coming up until you get there. If you think about the lines in a good song, you are taken along word by word, and the chorus becomes the repeat.

The layout has a central movement through the garden and across the terraces. There are choices to go left or right, taking the visitor through the space.

PATHWAYS AND STEPS

With this garden, one of the things I've done
a bit differently is to make quite a few of the paths
narrower than I normally would, largely so that
I don't lose planting space.

The main pathways are about 3ft (90–100cm) wide, but
for a number of those that we don't use every day, the
paths are even smaller. In the gravel garden, I've used
blocks made from the same stone I've used for paving.
To add a bit more interest, the paving has a textured finish,
and the stone blocks are quite smooth. Textual changes
like this are a subtle detail but can bring added interest.

As well as changing the size of the pathways, I also
altered the width of the steps that connect the lower
terrace and the first terrace. These were previously quite
narrow and made the space feel really tight, so I made
them broader to give enough room to be able to sit down
on them with a cup of tea or coffee. It also means I can
arrange pots on them, as a way of adding a few more
moments of interest as you walk around the garden.

There's a main path that goes right through the center
of the lawn, but I've isolated that by putting grass all the
way around it so that you step onto it, then you step off it.
The next set of steps sits to one side of the garage to help
pull the garage wall down into the garden. I have added
a couple of timber arches, which also add interest to the
movement through the spaces.

Once you've passed through the archway, there's
another series of little steps to your right that take you up
into the gravel garden. These are isolated blocks of stone,
each with plants all around them, so again, they serve
as another subtle indication that something different is
happening here. Then, as you enter the gravel garden,
another path leads to the greenhouse area and a little
woodland that wraps around it.

From the bottom to the top of the garden is probably
about 8ft (2.5m), so it is set on an old incline. I could have
opted for a simple path leading from one end of the
garden to the other, but by giving different treatment to
the steps, I have slowed down the route through the
garden, and I hope I have made it more interesting.

Designing any garden
layout is about controlling
the movement and
introducing commas
and full stops. Pathways,
steps, and gates help
you do that. For me,
movement through
any garden gives the
opportunity to add
detail and interest.

WALLS AND ARCHES

Adding planting to walls and arches is a simple way of helping connect the vertical elements down to the garden. The cottage really does suit climbing and rambling roses in particular.

Within my garden, the walls around the space are mainly created by the those of the garages and the retaining walls of the terracing. All of these walls are built from the same limestone as the house, which helps provide that sense of place. The only downside to this is that it's quite pale, so it reflects the light, which is great for north-facing aspects, but if you are facing south or southwest, it can be a bit bright. To counter this, every single one of those walls has been softened with plants to soak up the light and add to the overall atmosphere of the garden. For supports, I've used simple, discreet horizontal wires fixed to eyes screwed into the walls and trained up them all sorts of plants, including fanned fruit, roses, and different climbers.

One of my main intentions with the design of this garden is to encourage people to weave their way through the space rather than just going straight to the end, so I put in a couple of simple, nicely detailed timber arches along the way to break up the space. These are basically climbing frames for two beautiful English rambling roses, *Rosa* 'Malvern Hills'. They have soft, creamy-yellow flowers, and over time, they will start to hang down and soften the timber structure. Most of the roses I go for tend to carry good hips, so I don't cut these back. To encourage the birds, just above the arches sits one of the bird boxes I made for my previous book (*The Creative Gardener*). This year, some blue tits moved into it, and watching the birds flying in and out of it makes a lovely view from the gravel garden.

Rosa 'Malvern Hills' will eventually work its way up and over the arches onto the garage behind.

Clematis 'Bill MacKenzie'

Clematis 'Bill MacKenzie'

Height 13–26ft (4–8m) **Spread** 8–13ft (2.5–4m) **Time of flower** Summer–fall **Soil** Moist but well-drained **Position** Full sun/partial shade **Hardiness** Hardy

If I could only have one clematis, it would be this one! I was lucky enough to be gifted this by Waterperry Gardens, where the eminent gardener Valerie Finnis trained and raised the climber before showing it at an RHS show in 1976, where it won an Award of Merit. That history is as fantastic as the plant: It's a vigorous climber with fine-cut leaves. If left alone, it will reach up to 26ft (8m), but don't let that put you off, as you can prune it really hard. It's happy in sun or partial shade, and it does not seem picky when it come to soil. Great interplanted among larger roses. In midsummer, nodding lantern-shaped flowers with four rich, thick, yellow sepals cover the upper stems of the climber that have the look of the peel of citrus fruit, surrounded by darker stamens. These are followed by wonderful fluffy, silky seedheads that carry you through the winter months. I think the deciduous nature of the climber helps the winter display. All that and it's easy to grow, which can't be said about all clematis!

Holboellia coriacea

Holboellia coriacea

Sausage vine

Height 13–26ft (4–8m) **Spread** 8–13ft (2.5–4m) **Time of flower** Spring **Soil** Moist but well-drained **Position** Full sun/partial shade/full shade **Hardiness** Hardy

The first time I saw this plant—well, smelled it—I was wandering around a friend's garden and asked, "What's that?" "What?" he said. "That scent, it's lovely." "Oh, that's *Holboellia*." It covered his whole arbor and was still looking for places to go! He just kept walking, but I said, "No, no, stop, I need a bit more than that." He then waxed lyrical about the climber, which was introduced by E. H. Wilson in the early 1900s from China. It is highly scented and a little vigorous—but in a good way! The leaves are oblong, with a pointed tip, and evergreen, in a light to mid green, whose glossy appearance softens as the leaves mature but also darkens to a richer green and becomes more leathery. The twining stems are vigorous, so it's worth tying it in early, as it will attach itself to anything it crosses paths with. In later spring, it bears clusters of dangling flowers that vary in color, depending on the plant—on males, they are reddish-purple, on females, greenish-white. Some say it needs shelter, but it has done well for me in more open spots.

Clematis 'Bill MacKenzie'

Rosa 'Shropshire Lass'

Rose 'Shropshire Lass'

Height 13ft (4m) **Spread** 8–13ft (2.5–4m)
Time of flower Summer **Soil** Moist but
well-drained **Position** Full sun/partial
shade **Hardiness** Fully hardy

The older I get, the simpler my choice of
roses becomes; now, I really enjoy the
species roses and shrubs with simpler
flowers. Rose 'Shropshire Lass' was
introduced in 1968 as one of the first
climbers that David Austin bred, and it
became very important in his collection.
It's a climbing rose that is so simple and
just has a classy look about it. The foliage
is mid-green, and although it does only
flower once, don't let that put you off!
These flowers carry a wonderful fragrance
and are single and a blushed pink that
fades to white, with stamens that really
sing. In fall, the rose bears rich orange-red
hips that last well into the winter months,
which for me more than makes up for the
single flower show. It's happy in sun or
partial shade; I have it on a north wall,
and it's thriving, although the soil is
well mulched.

Rosa 'Shropshire Lass'

Rosa 'Madame Alfred Carrière'
Rose 'Madame Alfred Carrière'

Height 25ft (7.5m) **Spread** 8ft (2.5m) **Time of flower**
Summer **Soil** Moist but well-drained **Position** Full sun/
partial shade **Hardiness** Hardy

This is a beast of a climber, and you do need a little room
for it, but that said, it loves some hard pruning, so I have
grown it in smaller areas. Over the years, it has become a
a favorite for me on a large north wall; however, it does
seem as happy in the sun. It's an old rose that was

introduced in 1879 and is known for its strong fragrance,
which is quite sweet. The flowers are large and cup-
shaped and arrive in informal clusters, and while they're
usually a soft creamy white, they do on occasion carry a
flush of pink, varying in different lights. These bloom in
early summer and repeat, and if you want to encourage
these blooms right into October, keep deadheading the
dead flowers. This rose has always been reliable in my
garden, and the stems don't carry too many thorns.

Rosa MALVERN HILLS ('Auscanary' PBR)

Rose Malvern Hills

Height 15ft (4.5m) **Spread** 10–11½ft (3–3.5m) **Time of flower** Summer **Soil** Moist but well-drained **Position** Full sun/partial shade **Hardiness** Hardy

A David Austin introduction from 2000, this is a seriously hard-working plant. I think the first thing to say about this rambler is that it will flower more than once. The blooms arrive in clusters and will last well into fall, each nearly 2in (5cm) across and full double, in soft lemon fading to cream as the season moves on, with a light musk scent. The foliage seems strong and healthy, with a satin finish on stems that are flexible and more or less thornless. The rose can be pruned if you have more confined space and is happy in sun or partial shade. I have grown it over two arches, which I think suits its vertical growth. The hips are small but appear in good numbers, and they remind of hawthorn berries.

Ribes speciosum

Rosa MALVERN HILLS ('Auscanary' PBR)

Ribes speciosum

Fuchsia-flowered gooseberry

Height 6½ft (2m) **Spread** 5ft (1.5m) **Time of flower** Summer **Soil** Moist but well-drained **Position** Full sun/partial shade **Hardiness** Hardy

I think ornamental *Ribes* are valuable shrubs, as so many flower quite early in the year and offer up a good source of nectar to emerging insects. I love to see them when they are given room in wilder settings, and they are also super as part of a mixed hedge or as a single species. That said, *Ribes speciosum* is a little different and probably the most spectacular. The first time I saw one, it was being used as a wall shrub, which I think is a great way to grow it, as it seems to love that extra shelter the wall provides. Its branches were covered in lovely red, pendant-like flowers, which resemble small fuchsia flowers. They really stand out against the foliage. To start with, I did think it was a fuchsia, so I was pleased to find out later it is known as a fuchsia-flowered gooseberry—which is totally accurate! Its stems are on the prickly side, but I would call them graceful, with shiny, almost glossy green leaves that have a hint of the gooseberry about them. The foliage is nearly evergreen, and the flowers come alive in spring, followed by mini gooseberry-type fruits that are red in color and last for a good period of time. The shrub seems happy in sun or partial shade. If left to grow freely, it will reach up to 6½ft (2m) and seems to work in most soils.

PLANTING IN DRIFTS

A lot of people say that my garden looks like it's been there forever and that it feels so natural. The way that I have achieved this is to let things seed around and not be controlling, allowing plants to "drift" through the beds as they please.

Self-seeders are like fairy dust—you let them do their magic, then seedlings pop up wherever they want to, often in places you'd not necessarily think they would. If you look at how things work in nature, you understand that where plants put themselves is where they are at their happiest. Although putting in different layers of planting and playing with combinations are important in designing a garden, not everything needs to be perfectly organized. If you let go a little, you'll get some wonderful surprises.

The best way to do this is to learn which plants seed themselves around your garden and ask what they bring to the overall look. Have they got an interesting look, different flower shapes, good color? As with all plants, it's worth thinking about how well they perform as they go into the winter. Do they fade well, do they hold good shape, do they have interesting seedheads or berries?

Not all of us are going to get the same results with specific plants, as so much depends on the soil and conditions of where you live. That said, some, such as poppies and foxgloves, are renowned for self-seeding, so they are always worth trying. One plant that has worked particularly well in my garden is Baltic parsley (*Cenolophium denudatum*), which for some reason self-seeds around like crazy—so much so that I think I could supply enough for the RHS Chelsea Flower Show!

Achieving a "natural" look is mainly about being brave enough to leave your garden alone early in the year rather than going out there with a hoe and chopping up all the emerging self-sowers along with the weeds. Basically, it's a different way of gardening. Not everyone is comfortable with this method, and I usually end up having a "conversation" with Mrs. Frost, who gets concerned if there are too many things coming up that might be weeds.

Once you spot plants that have started seeding around, it's a case of being smart enough to leave the right amount of seedlings in situ. The others, you can pull out and plant in containers or give to friends. Sometimes, something will pop up in a random place, and I'll think, "Wow, that's amazing, I'm going to add more there," so I'll gather seed from other plants and scatter it in the same spot.

Collecting seeds is really simple—it's mainly a matter of doing it at the right time. Look out for when the seeds are ripe and gather them before they fall to the ground, preferably when they're already completely dry. You can hang plants upside down in a dry spot in paper bags, which will catch the seeds and keep off the dust. I then transfer the seeds to brown-paper envelopes and store them somewhere cool or, depending on the seeds, plant them right away, let them grow, then replant when they are larger seedlings.

I do tend to edit these plants throughout the season. I may clear an area and add something more permanent if it looks as if one place is a bit overcrowded. This usually lasts a week or so, then I'll get in and tease things out to get a better balance.

It's a good idea to get to know your weeds, so that you can distinguish them from the plants you want to keep and pull them out before they get established. As soon as true leaves emerge, you can start to tell what's what, and it's not really a long list of weeds that you seriously don't want in your garden—probably only about ten—the others you just don't want to let seed. As long as you're on top of those and continually pulling them out, you'll be fine.

There are still a few planting spaces in my garden, but you wouldn't think so because this is where I've allowed self-seeders to do their thing. Letting this magic happen is one of the best ways to not get bored with your garden.

Baltic parsley, poppy, and delphinium are all self-seeders that drive the ever-changing picture of my garden. They never grow in the same place, so the garden is always changing, which is quite charming.

Cenolophium denudatum
Baltic parsley

Height 3ft (1m) **Spread** 20in (50cm) **Time of flower**
Spring–early summer **Soil** Rich and fertile, but well-drained
Position Full sun/partial shade **Hardiness** Fully hardy

This is a very happy plant in my garden, as it seems
to love my drier conditions. It does appear to be
long-lived, and it seeds itself happily, needing only a
little management. I find that freedom really allows them
to bring something to the garden. My plants grow to
about 31–35in (80–90cm) tall. Interestingly, this is the
only member of its genus. I think it's quite a romantic
plant; the foliage is soft and fine-cut, rich green with a
silk finish. Its stems vary a little in color from a soft green
to a purple flush and, come June, they will carry pale,
umbillifer flowers that can look white or lime green
and that draw in a significant quantity of insects. After
flowering, the seedheads will last well into winter. It loves
a sunny spot, but it will work in semi-shade if that's all
you have. It seems happy in most soils, but don't let
them get too wet.

Delphinium requienii
Requin's larkspur

Height 3ft (1m) **Spread** 16in (40cm) **Time of flower**
Summer **Soil** Free-draining **Position** Full sun/partial
shade **Hardiness** Fully hardy

This delphinium offers something a little different. I first
saw this little star in the south of France, but when I got
back, I could not find it, until I came across it at a friend's
nursery (although, to be fair, the seed is readily available).
When I say "a little different," I mean you really will do a
double take when you see it. It's a biennial, but don't let
that put you off, as it can prolifically self-seed, so it works
like an annual. I have had them flower in the first year. I lift
and re-pot small seedlings and grow them elsewhere,
leaving a few to fill the remaining space. For me, they
work as well in the main borders as they do in the gravel
garden, and even in containers, and I find them quite
hardy. The plant has really good form, bushier than the
perennial types we grow, with branched spikes with a
loose feel. The stems bear leaves with a real shine to
them, which helps keep the slugs at bay, and masses of
large-spurred, exotic-looking, soft blue flowers. I have
planted it around *Euphorbia mellifera,* and the foliage
contrast is striking; they really do make a lovely couple.

Cenolophium denudatum

Delphinium requienii

Digitalis lutea
Straw foxglove

Height 35in (90cm) **Spread** 16in (40cm) **Time of flower**
Summer **Soil** Moist but well-drained **Position** Full sun/
partial shade/shade **Hardiness** Fully hardy

This is a great species of foxglove that comes true from
seed. Its leaves form a basal clump and are slender and
mid-green and carry a soft-sheen finish. From these
strong vertical stems are produced sets of two leaves
that repeat along their length, set at a quarter or half turn
from each other, which creates a series of crosses up the
stem. Come early June, this is topped off with delicate
spikes of creamy-yellow, trumpet-like flowers that have
a real elegance, which will keep on coming for a good
couple of months. Pollinating insects love them. I think
they still look interesting as they go to seed. It does look
a little special popping up through lower woodland
planting, where it will soon naturalize itself. It make great
bouquets for the house, so for me, it has become a handy
and reliable plant over the years.

Myrrhis odorata
Sweet cicely

Height 24–31in (60–80cm) **Spread** 3ft (1m) **Time of flower** Late spring–early summer **Soil** Most types **Position** Full sun/partial shade **Hardiness** Fully hardy

This is a little gem of a plant—it looks great but also works hard. It is known as sweet cicely, as the whole plant carries a sweet aniseed scent, and the leaves are great for adding sweetness to cooked fruit dishes. I use it a lot with rhubarb, and you can't believe how much it sweetens— and it's a lot better for you than a ton of sugar! I also think it makes a wonderful tea—it has a history of use as a medicinal herb. The plant has a lovely naturalistic feel, and being happiest in semi-shade, I like using it on the edge of woodland planting. When it starts to seed, it really guides you as to where it should grow, but if you are worried about it seeding too much, you could just clean it up after flowering. I have heard it called sweet bracken, which, for me, describes its fern-like, soft-green foliage. In late spring or early summer, the white, scented umbrella-shaped flowers arrive, carried on hollow tube-like stems. If you are happy to leave these after flowering, you will be blessed with near-black seeds that look incredible. The shape reminds me a little of rugby balls.

Papaver lateritium
Orange poppy

Height 20in (50cm) **Spread** 20in (50cm) **Time of flower** Summer **Soil** Moist but well-drained **Position** Full sun/partial shade **Hardiness** Fully hardy

My grandad was the chairman of his local British Legion, and every year we would attend the memorial service, and some years we would go to the Royal Tournament at Earl's Court and watch the Armed Forces compete. It was a big deal for my Grandad, and the poppy meant a lot—each year, he would buy me one. I have carried on doing this, which was why I started adding poppies to my garden, lest we forget! My grandad did like his orange marigolds, and *Papaver lateritium* provides a great splash of coppery-orange flowers. It loves dry, sunny conditions, so I use it in gravel planting, and it looks like a picture—mostly single flowers, but it does throw up the odd double. These sit on wiry, upright stems, and it just seems to keep flowering throughout the summer, so I just let it do its thing. It happily seeds around but never really becomes a problem—it's tough and not at all demanding. The foliage is a flat rosette of gray-green silky leaves that carry what seems like hundreds of fine hairs. The seed pods dry beautifully; I always think they would make great salt and pepper pots.

Papaver somniferum
Opium poppy

Height 3ft (1m) **Spread** 20in (50cm) **Time of flower** Summer **Soil** Moist but well-drained **Position** Full sun/ partial shade **Hardiness** Fully hardy

The other poppy I use a lot is the opium poppy—I'm not sure what my grandad would have thought of that! That said, we only seem to hear the negative side of this plant and its use in illegal drug production, but it is also used legally in opiates like codeine. On top of that, it is just a stunning plant. I let it do its thing and then clean it up the following spring. It offers great vertical presence in the garden, popping up through other plants. The flowers are large, open, and paper-like, in shades of pinks and purples, with some very rich in color. If you have a good number of these plants in the garden, the flowers will carry you through a couple of months and really pull in the insects. But it's not just the flower that I grow it for; the seed pods dry well in the garden and will last through the winter, so on a frosty day, they look lovely, and we also cut them for bouquets in the house.

POTS

I really like having plants in pots and containers around the garden; they are a simple way of creating different moments and different atmospheres and adding seasonal interest across the garden.

Plants in pots encourage people to stop, look, and generally slow down while moving around the garden. I often put pots on either side of steps, which was one of the reasons why I made the steps leading up to the main terrace extra wide (see page 86).

Pots also allow you to get more out of your garden. If you understand the microclimate of your plot, such as where it's particularly sheltered or exposed, you can choose the right plant for the right place. Growing in pots is a great way to experiment with and get to know a plant before committing to planting it in the garden. This method also gives you the opportunity—especially if you're addicted to plants, like me—to play around with combinations and create mini scenes across the garden. If you're going to put a collection of pots together, think about the backdrop for maximum impact.

Vacation pots

It seems to me that if you've got a flat garden, you want a sloping garden, but if you've got a sloping garden, you want a flat garden. It's the same thing if you're like me and love your plants. You're always thinking, "I wonder if I could make this or that work?"

One of the downsides of my work is the number of places I visit, the number of people I meet, and the number of conversations I have about plants. I've met a few people over the years who have been absolutely passionate about growing certain types of plants—whether it's tropical stuff, hostas, or succulents. You spend a day walking around their gardens with them, and they suck you into their world; they make it sound like it's easy, which often it's not. In reality, growing plants like these in containers can be a lot of hard work—digging things up, covering things up to protect them from frost and bad weather. Also, as I've gotten older, I've traveled a bit more to tropical and subtropical countries, and if there is a botanic garden there, I will drag Mrs. Frost around it. Of course, I take lots of photographs, and when I come home, I'll often try to grow something a bit more unusual that I've seen there.

I have a group of pots that I call my "vacation pots," in which I grow all the stuff I can't grow in the garden. These are exactly that, pots filled with plants inspired by my travels and visits to other people's gardens. Another reason I call them vacation pots is because I know at the end of the season, I'm going to have to move them somewhere sheltered, or put them in the greenhouse, so they get a little winter vacation as well.

I've probably got about 20–25 vacation pots, and I've placed them all in front of the office. All summer, if I'm working at home, I'll walk along the little path or sit out with a cup of tea, and the vacation pots are part of my life every single day. Having pots in a place where you observe them all the time means you remember to water them, unlike other pots that are more hidden away.

The pots provide a focal point and moment to pause on the way to the office. The plants look great against the horizontal timbers and the window frames.

Succulents in pots

I love succulents. They always remind me of my lovely Scruffy Nan, who used to collect all that sort of stuff in the 1970s, which was quite unusual at the time. I have strong memories of yuccas, cacti, and agave. As a kid growing up with a connection to the countryside, there's not much apart from the odd thistle and bramble that can really harm you, but these plants were really spiky and alien-looking. If you caught yourself on one of them, it hurt.

So, they've always fascinated me, and over the years, I've dipped in and out of growing them. Then, I had one of those typical gardeners' conversations with a couple of guys who'd set themselves up growing succulents, and before I knew it, I'd gotten sucked into growing them again and was off on another little adventure.

I grow these succulents in pots and always put them in places where you tend to stop and pause. We often think that a lot of those plants do best in really sunny conditions, but actually many of them don't and will scorch. I found a good spot on top of a wall that goes underneath the archway. It's like a wide shelf, so I've made an arrangement of pots there, and as you're going up the steps, you can look down on them. I sometimes use one as a centerpiece on an outdoor table or around the Japanese benches, placing them where I can sit, get up close, and better appreciate their detail. Because that's what they are—they're literally plants full of detail.

Each year, when I'm at certain garden shows, I'll find myself wondering if the guys are there and what new things I can get. One of the nurseries named a semponium (an aeonium bred with a sempervivum) 'Mrs. Frosty' after Sulina. The aeonium family are such quirky, fun-looking plants, great for dropping into borders to use sculpturally or to have fun with, as long as you remember to lift them and protect them before temperatures drop.

In some places, such as Yorkgate Garden, in Leeds, they plant aeoniums in the garden. But they use them more or less like bedding, planting them out in late spring and lifting them in late September/early October to store under cover. I've experimented with succulents by planting them in the gravel garden, but I have to admit, I haven't had much success, so I've gone back to putting them in containers filled with peat-free potting mix and a lot of sand. I suppose I'll still occasionally try a certain variety in the garden, as I can't help but constantly experiment. For the time being, though, as temperatures drop at the end of the year, I put all the pots back in the greenhouse. If I run out of space in the greenhouse, I'll set them next to a really sheltered wall and cover them with a fleece. The most important thing is to prevent these plants from getting wet over the winter, as it's the combination of wet and cold that can kill them off.

A broad retaining wall under the archway provides a great platform for the pots of succulents, and it's another way of slowing movement up and down the terraces.

Acer palmatum 'Bloodgood'

Japanese maple 'Bloodgood'

Height 13–16ft (4–5m) **Spread** 10–13ft (3–4m) **Time of flower** Spring **Soil** Moist, humus-rich but well-drained **Position** Partial shade/full shade **Hardiness** Hardy

When these trees started to arrive in Britain back in the 1800s, they must have created a stir, as they have been popular ever since! They carry a real elegance, and I have put a *palmatum* of some sort in every one of my own gardens. *Acer palmatum* was the first bit of Latin I ever learned at college, and I loved the logic of this word, meaning the palmate shape of the leaves, which describes them beautifully. At the time, I thought that was the coolest thing—sad, I know! I think

'Bloodgood' is one of the best dark-leaved Japanese maples; the leaves are so rich, a deep ruby-red color that lasts from spring to fall. Although not the most showy, the small purple flowers are followed by red fruit, which play their part as the fall color takes center stage and the ruby turns to crimson over the years. I even enjoy the leaves falling on the paved area below them, where they create a work of art. I have used this variety as a base woodland layer, as it does love a cool sheltered spot out of the midday sun. In my current garden, I have used one in a pot just as you open the gate, where it sits against a hornbeam hedge, and that contrast—wow, it just sings! It makes a great focal point and is one tree that will work well in a container, as it does not like

wet winter roots. Plus, it is not the quickest grower, so I re-pot it every couple of years and work toward the biggest pot I can practically have. If you are planting into the garden, just remember to choose a sheltered position and avoid heavy soil that waterlogs. I inherited one in the new garden, and it must have been there for a long time. It starts the year off really well, but it was planted in the wrong place, near a south-facing wall, so as we move into the heat of summer, the leaves start to scorch, and the poor tree does not look great. I haven't got the heart to remove it, though, so I just mulch it well and try to keep its roots as cool as I can. In my little courtyard, the dark-lobed leaves work well with the tree ferns and other woodlanders.

Agave celsii (Agave mitis)
Eastern dagger

Height 24in (60cm) **Spread** 20in (50cm)
Time of flower N/A **Soil** Well-drained
Position Sun **Hardiness** Not fully hardy

This is another plant that takes me straight back to Scruffy Nan's garden. She seemed to love plants from different parts of the world and over the years she also loved her pottery, so I think it was shapes and forms that caught her eye. There are about 200-odd species of *Agave*, and *A. celsii* is one from Mexico. One of the reasons I like growing this is it seems fairly hardy and copes with more water and shade than some other agaves—which is not a bad trait to have in this country! It forms rosettes of beautiful, blue-green, leathery leaves that remind me of an eastern desert, with edges that have small saw-like teeth. It will cope with a little more shade, but I place it in a sunny spot in well-drained, peat-free potting mix, with topsoil and a lot of sand. It will handle a fair amount of frost, and if you live in a warmer part of the country, placing your container near a warm wall and protecting it with fleece should be okay. It's most important to keep these plants dry in winter, as they really don't like very wet conditions.

Arisaema sp.
Cobra lily

Height 2½ft (80cm) **Spread** 10in (25cm)
Time of flower Spring–summer **Soil** Moist, humus-rich but well-drained **Position** Sun/partial shade **Hardiness** Hardy when established

Arisaemas seem to be an acquired taste, and if I'm honest, I wasn't sure about them when a friend sent me home with a few. To begin with, they were a little hit or miss, but then the more I learned about them, the more they started to fascinate me. They are tuberous perennials with two to three deeply cut, hand-like leaves, from which arise fascinating flowers in spring or early summer, with floppy, yellow-hooded spathes that protect the purple waxy spadix. The plants bulk up over time and can be long-lived. I thought I had lost them a few times, only for them to reappear in the compost bin after I'd disposed of them! I have tried to grow them in different ways: in pots partly planted into the ground; in my courtyard area, which is cooler and damper but not too wet in winter; and also in the woodland garden, where I treat them like bulbs, planting them to pop up among other plants. It's a plant that starts off male and becomes female as it matures.

Begonia sutherlandii
Sutherland begonia

Height 20–31in (50–80cm) **Spread** 20in (50cm) **Time of flower** Summer **Soil** Well drained in winter, moist in summer **Position** Partial shade **Hardiness** Hardy when established

Begonias take me back to my days working in the Parks Department and the bigger, bolder, brighter colors that we used in bedding schemes and hanging baskets. I now have quite a few begonias—a lot more subtle than where I began!—that I use in beds and in pots. For me, they add a little of the exotic. This particular begonia is from South Africa and has small, serrated leaves with red veins that are carried on red stems. It's a plant that will spread, producing soft orange flowers in the summer that carry on blooming late into the season. The tubers will get bigger over the years, and the plant reproduces from the bulbils on its stems in fall, just before it dies back. I have had young plants pop up among the gravel in my greenhouse floor. *Begonia sutherlandii* likes a cool, semi-shady spot but is not quite hardy enough to leave out in my garden, so it's one for vacation pots! That said, the tubers can be lifted and dried in the fall, then kept dry over winter.

Dahlia imperialis

Dahlia imperialis
Tree dahlia

Height 10ft (3m) **Spread** 5ft (1.5m) **Time of flower** Fall **Soil** Moist, humus-rich but well-drained **Position** Full sun **Hardiness** Tender

I had forgotten about the tree dahlia until I was filming in Wales a few years ago, where they were worked through a border. I had first seen them during my time in Devon, and it really took me back—they were stunning! The foliage can vary from green to the deeper colors and is a little aralia-like and deeply divided. These are carried on long, woody, bamboo-like stems and can make a real statement. The foliage alone warrants a place in a garden, and if you like your tropical plants, this will work very well. For me, flowering can be hit or miss; I need a very warm year, especially in the later part of summer, for the plant to bloom in early fall. The flower color can be variable, ranging from mauve to pale pink. I have even seen white flowers that carry a light orange central disc. I tend to grow mine in larger containers now and protect them in the winter. I have a friend who mulches well and leaves them in the garden over the winter, but I do think you need reasonably dry soil to do this.

Daphne × transatlantica PINK FRAGRANCE ('Blapink' PBR)
Daphne PINK FRAGRANCE

Height 20–31in (50–80cm) **Spread** 20–40in (50–100cm) **Time of flower** Spring, summer, fall **Soil** Moist but well-drained **Position** Sun/partial shade **Hardiness** Hardy

This is a shrub that I have found to be a little awkward over the years, as they do seem to be more finicky than your average plant! For instance, not all seem to even like being in containers. So, why do I put this in a container? First, to give me some time to really figure out where this beauty will be happy in the garden. Second, just to grow a little, as I have found that if the shrubs are a little more established, they do better for me. PINK FRAGRANCE is a lovely semi-evergreen, compact shrub with a bushy habit, making it great for a small space. The leaves are lance-shaped and green with a matte finish. As for the flowers, they are produced on new growth, with buds that are a deep pink opening to a lovely, soft, pale pink and carry a rich scent. When it comes to planting them, I add soil from my garden to my potting mix to make sure that I'm changing as little as possible for the plant. Although this daphne is hardy, they don't like exposed sites and prefer a sheltered spot away from cold winds and the midday sun. You need a good balance between moisture retention and good drainage so your plant doesn't sit in water over winter. These plants may take a little more thought and care to start with, but they will reward you for years.

Daphne x *transatlantica* PINK FRAGRANCE ('Blapink' PBR)

Echeveria agavoides 'Ebony'

Eucomis comosa 'Sparkling Burgundy'
Pineapple lily 'Sparkling Burgundy'

Height 20–31in (50–80cm) **Spread** 20in (50cm) **Time of flower** Summer **Soil** Well-drained **Position** Full sun **Hardiness** Half hardy (with protection over winter)

At first glance, you would be forgiven for thinking that these distinctive and unusual-looking plants would be hard to grow, but they are more than adaptable to our climate. The strap-like leaves emerge in spring in a deep burgundy color, but as the season progresses, they start to turn green. In midsummer, a thick, dark, upright stem emerges from the rosette of foliage, carrying what looks like an elongated purple pineapple! From this, purple-tinged flowers open that last for ages, which are followed by lovely architectural seedheads. During the growing season, I tend to liquid-feed a couple of times. Keep it in a sunny spot and make sure it does not dry out, and these exotic beauties will just do their thing.

Echeveria agavoides 'Ebony'
Echeveria 'Ebony'

Height 8in (20cm) **Spread** 16in (40cm) **Time of flower** Spring **Soil** Moist, humus-rich but well-drained **Position** Sun/partial shade **Hardiness** Hardy if dry

Echeverias for me are just sculptures—some of the forms are incredible. What's great is not just the diversity of species but that a lot of them will work indoors, so I tend to use mine in and out of the house. They also seem quite trouble-free and can withstand temperatures of below zero as long as they are not wet. Over the years, I have tucked them back under the eaves to keep the rain off and cover them with fleece. This one arrived on the scene in 2000 with a bit of a bang; it was popular from the start, and you can see why. It is a lovely succulent, with a rosette of leaves that are nearly triangular in shape, really fleshy and green in color, with tips up to a deep maroon, near-black in places. As a whole, the leaves form what for me looks a like a larger, fleshy-looking flower. Speaking of flowers, 'Ebony' produces a collection of single stems that carry small, soft, jewel-like flowers that have a yellow finish to their tips and hang delicately, adding a real elegance to the plant.

Eucomis comosa 'Sparkling Burgundy'

Hedychium spicatum
Spiked ginger lily

Height 5ft (1.5m) **Spread** 3ft (1m) **Time of flower** Summer–fall **Soil** Well-drained **Position** Partial shade **Hardiness** Hardy

This is a great member of the ginger family, one that I do leave in the garden over winter and mulch well, but I also grow it in pots—not only as a backup for if I lose one in the garden but because they have lovely foliage that is easy to arrange other plants against. Plus, this is one ginger that I find flowers more reliably. Where I live can have a cold start to the year, and gingers do generally take a while to get going. I have lost count of the number of times I have thought it's dead and then a few weeks later see a tiny vertical shoot pushing up through the ground. Stems carry elongated, pointed green leaves with a satin finish. To be fair, that is all I'm looking for when playing with collections of pots. In late summer most years, spikes of pale creamy-yellow and at times nearly white flowers are held above the foliage. These have a sweet scent, and as these fade, they are followed by green seedheads that ripen in warmer years and open to reveal orange linings and red seed pods. This plant loves a well-drained potting mix, so I use sand, soil, and peat-free potting mix roughly in equal parts. I do feed them a couple of times through the year and keep them well watered.

Hosta 'Dilithium Crystal'
Hosta 'Dilithium Crystal'

Height 6in (15cm) **Spread** 20in (50cm) **Time of flower** Summer **Soil** Moist, humus-rich but well-drained **Position** Partial shade/full shade **Hardiness** Hardy

I know a lot of people ask what the point is of growing hostas, as they are like caviar to slugs, but I do think the thicker-leaved plants deter them. I do love this hosta, as it forms a wonderful little mound of slimy tongues with blue foliage, and it works really well in a container. The leaves have a subtle curve to them and look great after a rainshower. Hostas are not really known for their flowers, but these are quite cute; they are purple, which pops against the foliage. Mine start flowering in late June and carry on into early July, lasting for a good eight weeks. It is a hosta that will scorch if positioned in direct sun, so it's best grown in semi- or full shade.

Impatiens omeiana

Impatiens omeiana
Mount Omei busy Lizzie

Height 24in (60cm) **Spread** 20in (50cm) **Time of flower**
Late summer **Soil** Moist, humus-rich but well-drained
Position Dappled/partial shade **Hardiness** Tender

A pot for a damp, shady spot. Most think of impatiens as
"busy Lizzie," which we seemed to say endlessly at the
Parks Department, but there are some lovely species
from around the world, and *omeinia* really does catch the
eye. The foliage is quite exotic and adds flair to planting
schemes, looking especially wonderful with the larger
foliage of hostas, ferns, or podophyllums. There are
varying reports of how vigorously it will spread, so
watch it closely to make sure its behavior is within your
comfort zone, or grow it in pots to restrict its growth.
This species hails from China and has vertical red stems
carrying slightly serrated, narrow green leaves with a
creamy yellow midrib that looks as if it is sipping into the
main leaf. Come mid- to late summer, soft creamy-yellow
flowers sit above the foliage. It does not like to dry out
and wants a shady spot. Come winter, mine goes into the
greenhouse for protection, but if you live in a really mild
area, you might be okay to leave it out—just do a little
research first.

Musa sikkimensis 'Red Tiger'

Musa sikkimensis 'Red Tiger'

Darjeeling banana 'Red Tiger'

Height 10–15ft (3–4.5m) **Spread** 6½–10ft (2–3m) **Time of flower** Summer–fall **Soil** Well-drained **Position** Full sun/partial shade **Hardiness** Half hardy (with protection over winter)

If you are putting a collection of vacation pots together, a banana is not a bad place to start. It promises you tall, upright stems with large leaves, which allow you to build contrasts. *Musa sikkimensis* 'Red Tiger' is a little different and does elicit a comment or two. I love watching the leaves as much as I do the crosiers on tree ferns. It is found in the Himalayas and really is a stunning plant, with good upright growth and paddle-like leaves that develop maroon-striped markings and carry a dark maroon-red underside. I love the young leaf growth and its deep red coloring. It is happy in sun or partial shade and out of the wind when it becomes winter. It is not hardy—I even have to wrap it in the greenhouse—but it is well worth the extra work. I don't water my plants over the winter; I just check them in the spring to see if they need potting or just resume watering again. I then feed them in late spring before moving them back outside for the growing season after the last frost.

Tinantia pringlei

Mexican wandering Jew/spotted widow's tears

Height 8in (20cm) **Spread** 24–31in (60–80cm) **Time of flower** Summer–fall **Soil** Well-drained **Position** Full sun **Hardiness** Hardy

This is a real dazzler that was collected from northwest Mexico and that I have been growing for the last couple of years—and it's thriving. That said, I have not risked leaving it out over winter so far, but I have been told it can handle low temperatures, and it does seem to go seed quite easily. So, for these reasons, for me, it's another good candidate for a container. This alpine perennial has lovely shield-shaped, mid-green leaves with a dark maroon marking that looks like blotches of ink, which look really good against aeoniums. The underside carries the darker tones of the wiry stems with a wonderful lined detail and a small, delicate, soft lavender-colored flower. It seems to spread easily, and I think it could make a good little groundcover. It loves the sun and a soil with good drainage.

Tinantia pringlei

Container ponds

I brought lots of things with me from my previous house, including some big water containers that I use to create pause points in the garden. They are pause points not just for me but also for wildlife, as they provide a source of water and are great for creating a habitat for insects, birds, and animals.

I've got a couple of little tanks up near the greenhouse—one outside the office and one down on the main terrace, which contains a simple water lily (*Nymphaea*). Growing this plant in a tank is really easy, as I can simply lift out the basket containing the water lily or empty the tank if need be. Technically, the tank is too small for the lily (and it fills the space beautifully), so periodically—more or less once a year—outside the growing season when they are dormant, I'll take the plant out, divide it up, and put one part back, and then someone I know gets a water lily starter. If the plant looks too congested at any other time. I take it out of its pot, tease it apart with a couple of garden forks, then replant the parts in baskets again with an aquatic soil topped with gravel before lowering it back into the water.

If you are planting a water lily for the first time, always position them in semi-shade and don't put them in their final depth immediately, as this can shock and kill the plant. It's far better to lower it in incrementally by sitting the basket on a brick "plinth" that sits 8in (20cm) or so below the water surface, gradually submerging it deeper into the water over the course of the growing season.

Top to bottom: Use two forks back to back to divide a large water lily.

Repot your divided water lilies into pots of aquatic soil.

Lower the lily in its new pot into the container before filling with water.

Positioned on the lower terrace, the bog container is a great little talking point, as it's not what people are expecting. It's happiest in partial shade, which is why I chose to put it on the north-facing side of the house.

Bog container

This is literally a container that's filled with bog plants. Why wouldn't I want to just give them a try, even if I live in an incredibly dry part of the country? Maybe it's just the feeling that the grass is always greener?

Obviously, when I'm on a stage somewhere or I'm on TV, I often preach about using the right plant in the right place... then I go off to garden shows and visit lots of nurseries and, because I'm a plantaholic, when I see these little beauties, I can't resist. I find myself tempted and thinking maybe I can create these mini worlds in containers, and if I make sure the plants are in the right conditions, then I don't have to stress too much.

If I'm honest, it's probably because these containers bring to mind lots of memories of my time living in Devon and are a way to replicate its damp environment. In particular, I have a memory of going down to Doone Valley in early spring and looking at the bracken, then getting into the water and seeing all the wonderful shapes and forms of the marginal plants. If you love certain plants and you've developed connections with them, it's natural to want to try to grow them. Discovering new plants, researching and finding ways to grow them, takes you on a little journey; you disappear into another world. My bog container was born of that thought process.

I've used an old galvanized bathtub, the sort that my nan used to put me in occasionally in front of the old fire—that's how old I am! I drilled some holes into the bottom of it so that excess water could drain away, then simply filled it with a mix containing peat-free compost, soil, composted bark, and some sand. Then, it was just a matter of planting it with plants that like bog conditions.

I had a lot of fun finding miniature versions of all the things that I'd connected to in the wild in Devon. My decisions weren't so much driven by color as by choosing lots of different shapes and forms. There are little ferns in there, gunneras, and rodgersias.

Gunnera magellanica
Devil's strawberry

Height 4in (10cm) **Spread** 12in (30cm)
Time of flower Summer **Soil** Damp, boggy
Position Partial shade **Hardiness** Hardy

This dwarf cousin of the larger gunnera forms a lovely mat of small, textured, crinkle-edged, dark-green leaves. Each leaf is compact and only about an inch across. It's very useful and an attractive way to cover a damp spot. One of the reasons why I grow it in a pot is because I can't provide that perfect spot. In milder parts of the country, you may find the plant works as an evergreen; this isn't the case for me, but it will survive a cold winter if the weather is not too wet. The female plants carry tiny green flowers that are followed by spherical orange to bright red fruit—it does require a male plant in close proximity in order to fruit, though.

Gunnera perpensa
River pumpkin

Height 35in (75cm) **Spread** 35in (75cm)
Time of flower Late summer **Soil** Damp, boggy **Position** Partial shade/full shade
Hardiness Hardy

Gunnera is a plant that so many of us know as a giant of a thing, so much so that it is now viewed as a pest in parts of the country. I, for one, do not have room for the large *Gunnera manicata*, which I look upon as the big brother of the short variety, *Gunnera perpensa*. This plant is quite vigorous when it gets established, but it is not always great in very cold areas, which is one of the reasons why I grow it in a pot. The other is that in my garden, I really do not have the damp conditions they love. This plant is clump-forming, with leaves that are more or less kidney-shaped and look heavily grained, which provides a lovely texture. Spikes of reddy-brown flowers come up through the foliage. Another thing I love about these plants is that they have been around for millions of years and belong to one of the oldest angiosperm families. That is crazy!

Iris laevigata 'Royal Cartwheel'
Iris 'Royal Cartwheel'

Height 24in (60cm) **Spread** 8in (20cm)
Time of flower Summer **Soil** Damp, moist
Position Sun/partial shade **Hardiness** Fully hardy

It's crazy to think that as a group, irises can range from drought-tolerant, dry-loving perennials, to marsh lovers, to sun-loving plants, to ones that will tolerate shade. *Iris laevigata* is one that would be found growing happily in shallow waters and boggy ground. I do find it fascinating that it has been cultivated in Japan for more than a thousand years, and some varieties that are still available today are mentioned in early Japanese gardening books. For me, 'Royal Cartwheel' is one of the best; it has upright, sword-like, mid-green leaves, and come May or June, it bears beautiful violet-blue flowers that carry a white strip to the center of each petal, creating a stunning effect. If you plant these close to water, you will also soon see it is a favorite of bees, butterflies, and even dragonflies.

Polystichum setiferum 'Congestum'

Soft shield fern

Height 10in (25cm) **Spread** 8in (20cm)
Time of flower N/A **Soil** Moist but well
drained **Position** Full sun/partial shade
Hardiness Fully hardy

This is a favorite evergreen fern. I do
like *Polystichum* in general—and we do
have a few!—and while this one is mini
compared to others, that does not
take away from its grace. The foliage
is mid-green, and the fronds are tight,
upright, and really finely cut, which creates
this lovely feathery texture. *Polystichum
setiferum* 'Congestum' is native to the cool
and moist regions of Western Europe, and
that does seem to be its happy place. That
said, it does seem to do okay when the
conditions are a little drier. It only gets to
about 10in (25cm) high, so it's really good
for working into a shady little gap. It's not
the quickest grower, but that's not a bad
thing. This is another plant that I would
mulch to help retain moisture and regulate
the soil temperature.

Polystichum setiferum 'Congestum'

Rodgersia 'Bronze Peacock'

Rodgersia 'Bronze Peacock'

Height 20–40in (50–100cm) **Spread** 28in (70cm) **Time of flower** Summer **Soil** Moist but well-/poorly drained **Position** Full sun/ partial shade **Hardiness** Fully hardy

I love it in spring when the reddish-bronze foliage of this plant starts to emerge from the ground, but it also looks great throughout the whole growing season, and the sculptural form of the plants makes them great to plant against. The chestnut-shaped leaves are thick and textured, looking more or less metallic, with a shine that seems to catch the sun. They will fade to green later on but remain edged with color. If you stand back and look at these plants, you can see where the name "peacock" comes from, as the leaves do look a little like a fanned tail. Trusses of pink flowers sit above the foliage on strong red stems. Rodgersia is a plant that does love a little moisture, but it will do okay in good soil once it gets itself established—I mulch mine well if they are planted in the garden. If they are really happy, the plants could get to 3ft (1m) (although they don't for me), and they will clump up over time.

Trollius x cultorum 'Alabaster'

Giant buttercup or globeflower

Height 24in (60cm) **Spread** 12in (30cm) **Time of flower** Late spring–early summer **Soil** Moist but well-drained, fertile **Position** Sun/partial shade **Hardiness** Fully hardy

This herbaceous perennial just makes me smile. I used it at the RHS Chelsea Flower Show in 2013 and fell in love with it there. I plant it with Iris sibirica 'Tamberg' and Aruncus dioicus 'Horatio' next to water, and it just sings! It's got a charm to it, plus you don't see it all over. If you spot a bee popping into the cream-colored, buttercup-like flowers, you will be hooked. This plant thrives in a damp position—that said, I have gotten away with planting it in drier spots, but only where the soil has been in very good shape and out of full sun. The lobed green foliage clumps slowly, and the flowers are a stunning globe shape, with a dominant central boss of upright petals. It is a plant whose spent blooms I will let Mrs. Frost deadhead regularly for a longer display of flowers.

I often preach about using the right plant in the right place, but then I go off to garden shows and visit lots of nurseries, and, because I'm a plantaholic, when I see these little beauties, I can't resist.

THE GARDENER

Working as an apprentice gardener in a parks department in Devon taught me all the traditional rules of how and when we should maintain a garden. We were taught all this really technical stuff and processes for absolutely everything. Obviously, we were graded on what we'd learned, and no one ever said, "Oh, you might not always do it this way"; or, "This is what we do in the southwest, but it'll be different in other parts of the country." None of that was ever explained. It was literally a case of check the box for when to prune this and check the box for how you're going to do it. So, I became technically proficient and learned everything that I needed to know as a parks gardener, but it wasn't until I went to work for Geoff Hamilton that I realized there was more to gardening than I'd ever imagined. Geoff taught me not to stick rigidly to "rules" and instead to take time to observe a garden and be more reactive to what plants need from me.

Go at your own pace

So, with Geoff's insight, I changed my mindset about maintenance being all about control and making things look neat and tidy and realized it's actually about guiding, nurturing, and playing your part where you need to, but also knowing when to back off and let nature do its thing.

In many ways, gardening is really simple—at the heart of it is understanding your site and what your plants need and reacting accordingly. By this, I mean *really* understanding the site in as much detail as you can: knowing how the sun moves through the space; where there is shade, rain shadows, sheltered and exposed spots, and microclimates (I've got a lot of limestone walls, and the south-facing ones retain the sun's warmth in the stones); soil types, and also how all of those things can change. There will be an array of temperature levels within even a small garden, there will be plants that can better handle cooler conditions than others, and there will be some that may need a bit more help to get through the winter months.

This knowledge comes from close observation of your garden over time. Lots of people tell me that they haven't got time to do this, as they are too busy, but they are missing the point. If you sit down with a cup of tea and maybe a notebook or a camera, and you really look at what's going on in your space, the reality is that it will start to tell you what to do. It's really worth doing this, even if you've had the same garden space for years.

We should not be chasing perfection in our gardens, as they change all the time! For me, it's about making the most of the atmosphere in every part of your garden and how it affects you.

Cutting back the old, supportive stems of the *Disporum* in late spring.

In the past, I would always do certain jobs at specific times, and if you look at all the old gardeners' sayings, what you did in the garden would often be linked to particular social dates in the British calendar. When I was a kid, gardening with my nans and grandads each month was linked to specific tasks, because for them, this way of gardening set the rhythm for the year. We can't rely on that now; climate change means this rhythm has been broken. Nowadays, do we really know what must be done in January? Or in February? I'm writing this in April, and it's freezing cold, and we've just had a really, really wet winter. I've been living in Lincolnshire since I was 21—so 30-odd years—and I've seen my local river overflow more in the last 10 years than I did in the 20 years previous. So, it's important to understand that we just can't maintain gardens the way we used to.

This idea of letting go of that traditional rhythm also ties in with me being more relaxed about garden jobs. I am guided by the day-to-day weather to determine my maintenance schedule, and I'm more reactive; if I see something in dire need of help, I give it some help, but if it's happy, I leave it alone. I tend to think that if a job doesn't get done in January, it'll get done in February; and if doesn't get done in February, no stress—I'll do it at another time, or next year. That said, Mrs. Frost still wants everything to look neat and tidy, which does cause the occasional disagreement in our household, so we have to come to a compromise.

My approach to weeds is a good example of going at my own pace. I garden organically, so the only way I can get rid of weeds is to pull them by hand, but these days, I don't tend to be too fussy about the odd one coming up here and there. You can take a little more relaxed approach here, as there are lots of weeds that you don't need to be overly worried about, such as annuals. These are generally easy to keep on top of if you regularly pull them out, hoe them down, and make sure they don't release seeds. More pernicious perennial weeds, such as bindweed and couch grass, do need a little more attention, though, and I always take them out by hand. I've got a couple of gardening friends who tackle pernicious weeds by planting annuals quite heavily in the same area so that the weeds have to compete for space, light, and nutrients. They know that the annuals will occupy the space nicely over the summer months, and then they can clear the weeds along with these when they have finished. Plus, it means they can clear a larger area rather than having to work around existing plants.

Pruning is another gardening job that seems to carry a bit of a fear factor, but I like to keep it simple. Yes, of course, for some plants, pruning can stimulate growth so they produce better flowers and fruit, but I tend to administer a light touch, removing only dead, diseased, or damaged growth. I may also prune to thin a plant's stems and guide a shape, but most of that is done when I have the time. Cutting back dead growth on perennials at the end of the season was traditionally done as a way of "putting the garden to bed" for the winter, but now you are better off leaving them in place, as seedheads and berries will provide a great source of food for birds and other wildlife.

By growing plants and watching them over the years, by trusting your instinct rather than being prescriptive, you will build up your understanding of when you can break certain "rules," which means you can relax into whatever you're doing, and if there's a risk to be taken, it will be a slightly more calculated one. It's a bit like having children... I've got four, and the way you treat the first one is very different than how you treat the fourth. I'm the same with the garden—I am far more relaxed as the years go by.

Overall, I feel we all just need to think more about the reasons why we're doing maintenance in the garden. For me, the logic is that if you put the work into the soil, mostly everything else will fall into place.

Looking after the soil
Without doubt, some of the most important things Geoff taught me were not to use peat and to care for the soil. The soil is everything; it's the foundation in which your whole garden is built; rather like the foundations of a house, it is a cost that you do not see, but everything will eventually collapse if you don't get it right. Love your soil, understand your soil, and gardening just becomes easier.

So, for example, if you live in a limestone area with a soil pH that is alkaline and you want a lot of acid plants... you'll need to move. Don't make work for yourself by fighting your soil and conditions. Be practical, learn to love your soil, and grow what will be happy in it. By all means improve it, but don't waste time trying to radically change it.

When we arrived in this garden, the soil was lifeless—it was like dust and just fell through your fingers. Even when I dug into the ground, there was little, if any, sign of worms or life—just weed after weed after weed. Sorting out the soil was the first job, and I started off

Preparing a bed
with a good mulch
of well-rotted
farmyard manure.

by digging every border I created and then incorporating well-rotted manure. I know there's a lot of debate about whether to dig or not to dig and the impact doing so has on soil structure, but I prefer to dig everywhere once in a new space, as it helps me understand how the soil varies around the garden, and I can get the first lot of mulch in. In that first year, I mulched most of the garden at least twice. That might seem like a huge time and financial commitment, but I could get it done while in the planning stage, and the soil really needed those extra nutrients and texture. In the second year, I mulched the garden again—a lot of it twice.

The best soil improver is good old-fashioned well-rotted manure. We live in the countryside, so it's easy to get hold of this locally, but if you can't get it, you can use composted bark, homemade compost, or dead mushroom compost. Over the years, whatever size garden I've had, I've always tried to make my own compost. I really enjoy the process, and it's great from an environmental level, in that as little as

It's tempting to mulch and spread chicken pellets around the whole area, but not every plant needs this. So, as time moves on, I tend to mulch and feed only the hungrier plants.

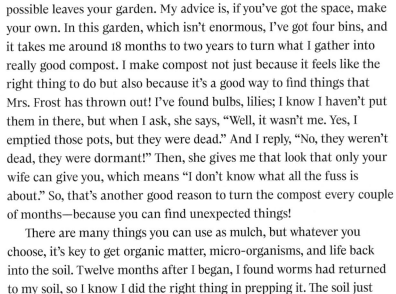

possible leaves your garden. My advice is, if you've got the space, make your own. In this garden, which isn't enormous, I've got four bins, and it takes me around 18 months to two years to turn what I gather into really good compost. I make compost not just because it feels like the right thing to do but also because it's a good way to find things that Mrs. Frost has thrown out! I've found bulbs, lilies; I know I haven't put them in there, but when I ask, she says, "Well, it wasn't me. Yes, I emptied those pots, but they were dead." And I reply, "No, they weren't dead, they were dormant!" Then, she gives me that look that only your wife can give you, which means "I don't know what all the fuss is about." So, that's another good reason to turn the compost every couple of months—because you can find unexpected things!

There are many things you can use as mulch, but whatever you choose, it's key to get organic matter, micro-organisms, and life back into the soil. Twelve months after I began, I found worms had returned to my soil, so I know I did the right thing in prepping it. The soil just seemed to have digested the manure, but I won't do this every year, I'll monitor how it looks, feels, and smells and how the plants are growing.

Keep an eye on your soil and feed it only if you feel the plants need a boost. You don't have to blanket everything—you can just mulch specific areas. In terms of what time of year to mulch, it depends on where you are in the country. If you live somewhere wet, the window of opportunity is quite short, and you're probably looking at March to May. We live in a really dry area and often mulch from September all the way through to May. However, certain areas in the garden get wetter than others, and this affects what I do. For example, the soil at the top of the garden is more free-draining, so I worked it at the start of my mulching window—September/October—whereas the soil near the house was mulched in early April.

Occasionally, in spring, I'll sprinkle organic chicken pellets around if I think something needs a bit more feed. In simple terms, trees, shrubs, and roses generally benefit from a bit of extra feed, but many herbaceous perennials perform better on fewer nutrients. If they are overfed, they can grow too quickly and have weak, sappy, green growth that is prone to falling over and attack from pests and diseases.

I'm convinced that once you get your soil in a good place, the rest sort of happens. Caring for your soil is the single most important thing you can do to have healthy plants and a beautiful garden.

PLANT SUPPLIERS

We are very lucky in this country to be blessed with some fantastic growers and suppliers, and I'm lucky enough to call so many of them friends. Most of the plants in this book have come from the suppliers listed below. Thank you to each of them for their support and shared knowledge over the years.

Alchemy Ferns alchemyferns.co.uk

Avon Bulbs avonbulbs.co.uk

Barcham Trees barcham.co.uk

Beth Chatto's Plants and Gardens bethchatto.co.uk

Branch Nurseries branchnurseries.co.uk

Daisy Roots daisyroots.com

Deepdale Trees deepdale-trees.co.uk

Edulis edulis.co.uk

Hardy's Cottage Garden Plants hardysplants.co.uk

Hare Spring Cottage Plants harespringcottageplants.co.uk

Hillier Trees trees.hillier.co.uk

Hooksgreen Herbs hooksgreenherbs.com

Kelways kelways.co.uk

Kevock Garden Plants kevockgarden.co.uk

Kitchen Garden Plant Centre
    kitchengardenplantcentre.co.uk

Knoll Gardens knollgardens.co.uk

Lindum turf.co.uk

Marshalls Seeds marshallsgarden.com

Moore & Moore Plants mooreandmooreplants.co.uk

New Forest Hostas & Hemerocallis newforesthostas.co.uk

Peter Beales Roses classicroses.co.uk

Pheasant Acre Plants pheasantacreplants.co.uk

Robinson Seeds & Plants mammothonion.co.uk

Surreal Succulents surrealsucculents.co.uk

Swines Meadow Farm Nursery
    swinesmeadowfarmnursery.co.uk

INDEX

ACKNOWLEDGMENTS

Author acknowledgments

First, thanks to everyone who has played their part in my gardening life: for your help, time, knowledge, and friendship. It really is a wonderful world.

As for this book, thank you to Chris for your friendship and believing in me when it comes to this writing malarky! Ruth for making me believe—I will listen to you more in the future, I promise! Barbara for just being you. Christine and Lucy for pulling the book together with Barbara, of course. Jason not just for the amazing photos but the laughs along the way. You are all stars.

Then there is my team, who are great, well, most of the time. Abbie-Jade for just keeping on, the odd photo, and wearing all the hats you do! Polly and Jane for work on the plans, and Ash the cat for agreeing to be on the cover—he enjoys working with Jason, too! And thank you to those who helped me more than they will ever know during the tough times: Gary Broadhurst, my BBC exec, and Theia, my agent. I will never forget what you both did for me.

Lastly, thank you to all the people who have and do create music. I have used the songs in this book to drive an atmosphere and emotion, and I've spent a lifetime interpreting lyrics, many of which have become personal to me. I have used music to help me in so many ways: to reflect, cry, dream, dance, smile, make sense of things, and even sing, badly!

Warm love to you all. xx

Publisher acknowledgments

DK would like to thank Abbie Frost for all her help, Polly Hindmarch and Jane Adams for the planting plans, Jem Marryat for drone photography, John Tullock for US consulting, Kathy Steer for proofreading, Lisa Footitt for indexing, Adam Brackenbury for cover repro, and Steve Crozier for image retouching.

Picture credits

The publisher would like to thank the following for their kind permission to reproduce their photographs:
(Key: a-above; b-below/bottom; c-centre; f-far; l-left; r-right; t-top)

Alamy Stock Photo: David Perry 51tc, John Richmond 179tl; **Dreamstime.com:** Happywindow 125bl, Tom Meaker 125tl; © **Frank P Matthews:** 50tl; **Abbie Frost:** 9, 10, 11, 14-15, 24tc, 26br, 31tl, 44tr, 49, 50tc, 61tl, 62br, 66bc, 77tr, 79tr, 81tr, 84-85t, 91tc, 95bl, 101bl, 106bl, 109tr, 109br, 110tr, 135tr, 137tr, 138, 141br, 150tr, 163tr, 176tl, 181tl; **Adam Frost:** 21, 37, 59, 64br, 74, 119, 130; **GAP Photos:** Thomas Alamy 146, Richard Bloom 137bc, Richard Bloom - Rod and Jane Leeds garden, Suffolk 47bl, 148, Christina Bollen 47tl, Jonathan Buckley 160bl, Chris Burrows 91tl, Torie Chugg 160tr, 178br, Tim Gainey 122tl, Claire Higgins 51tr, Martin Hughes-Jones 147bl, 175tr, Zara Napier 97tc, Clive Nichols - Hook End Farm, Berkshire 97tr, Howard Rice 79bl, 99tr, Stocks and Green 45, Graham Strong 25tl; **Jason Ingram:** 25tr, 31cr, 31bl, 40br, 50tr, 63, 66tl, 78bl, 90tc, 90tr, 91tr, 101tr, 141tl, 141tr, 180; **Marianne Majerus Garden Images:** © MMGI / Marianne Majerus 147tr; **Victoriana Nursery Gardens / Stephen Shirley:** 51tl

All other images © Dorling Kindersley Limited

Editorial Manager Ruth O'Rourke
Project Editor Lucy Philpott
US Executive Editor Lori Hand
Senior Designer Barbara Zuniga
Jacket Coordinator Emily Cannings
Senior Production Editor Tony Phipps
Senior Production Controller Stephanie McConnell
DTP and Design Coordinator Heather Blagden
Art Director Maxine Pedliham

Editorial Juliet Roberts, Helena Caldon
US Editor Heather Wilcox
Design Christine Keilty
Photography Jason Ingram

First American Edition, 2025
Published in the United States by DK Publishing,
a division of Penguin Random House LLC
1745 Broadway, 20th Floor, New York, NY 10019

A catalog record for this book is available from the Library of Congress.
ISBN: 978-0-5938-4426-7

DK books are available at special discounts when purchased in bulk for sales promotions, premiums, fund-raising, or educational use. For details, contact: DK Publishing Special Markets, 1745 Broadway, 20th Floor, New York, NY 10019
SpecialSales@dk.com

Printed and bound in Malaysia
www.dk.com

This book was made with Forest Stewardship Council™ certified paper—one small step in DK's commitment to a sustainable future. Learn more at **www.dk.com/uk/information/sustainability.**

To Sulina, my wife (Mrs. Frost), Abbie-Jade, Jacob, Amber-Lily, and Oakley: You have all had a lot to deal with in the last few years, and I'm so very proud of you all and love you more than I think you will ever understand. Thank you for helping me become a better person and helping me find my place in the world—I'm a lucky man. xxx

ABOUT THE AUTHOR

Adam Frost is an award-winning garden designer, with seven Royal Horticultural Society (RHS) Chelsea Flower Show Gold Medals to his name. He is a presenter on BBC *Gardeners' World* and BBC coverage of the RHS Flower Shows.

Gardens have always been a major part of Adam's life. He began gardening as child while growing up in Essex and was greatly influenced by his grandparents. He started his horticultural training with the North Devon Parks Department before working for the great organic gardener and TV presenter Geoff Hamilton. Adam went on to set up his own company, designing gardens across the world. He has written four books and is a popular public speaker.

Adam is married to Sulina and has four kids, two dogs, and Ash the cat, living in Lincolnshire. Alongside gardening and family life, he loves music, cooking, and sports, particularly soccer. Today, gardens are a place to connect and spend time with family and friends, cooking, having fun, and creating new memories.